The Mini Manual of Zodiac Signs

First published by Parragon in 2010
Parragon
Queen Street House
4 Queen Street
Bath BA1 1HE, UK

Page layout by Stonecastle Graphics Ltd.

ISBN 978-1-4075-9361-6

Printed in China

The Mini Manual of

Zodiac Signs

Bath • New York • Singapore • Hong Kong • Cologne • Delhi • Melbourne

CONTENTS

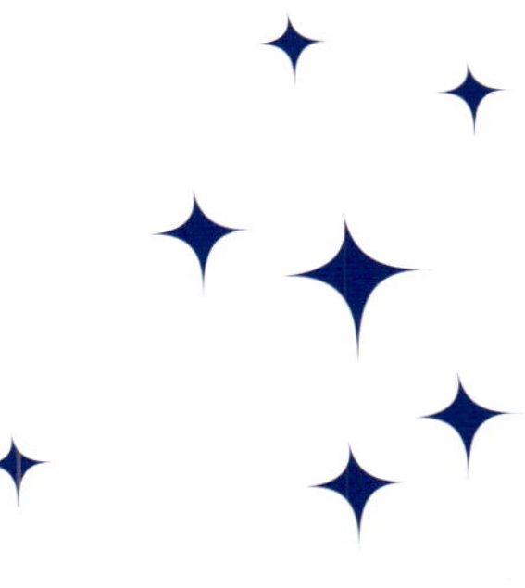

NTRODUCTION

Most of us know our astrological sign, although we often call it our star sign. Our astrological sign the sign that the Sun occupied at the time of our rth. The term "star sign" is a reference to the twelve nstellations in the zodiac. However, this can be rather isleading! The astrology practiced in the West is more ncerned with planets than stars. It focuses on the ght planets in our solar system (Mercury, Venus, Mars, piter, Saturn, Uranus, Neptune, and Pluto), plus the n and the Moon, which it also considers to be planets, though astrologers are well aware that these are t really planets. Yet terminology doesn't affect the trological influence of these very important heavenly dies.

The zodiac is an elliptical belt of sky around the Earth at contains the twelve constellations—Aries, Taurus, emini, Cancer, Leo, Virgo, Libra, Scorpio, Sagittarius, apricorn, Aquarius, and Pisces. Every year, from our ntage point on Earth, the Sun appears to move rough each constellation in turn, spending about thirty ys in each one. So when the Sun journeys through Leo, bies born at that time will have a Leo astrological sign.

This book is an introduction to the twelve astrological ns, describing their general characteristics, how ey behave in love, their career potential, the way they ndle money, and how they can stay healthy. There is o a list of places and things ruled by each sign, and scriptions of how the signs get on with one another.

PLACES AND THINGS RULED BY EACH ZODIAC SIG

THE WORLD OF ARIES

CITIES	Athens, Birmingham, Florence, Naples
COUNTRIES	Denmark, England, Germany
COLOR	Red
NUMBER	One
DAY OF THE WEEK	Tuesday
GEMSTONE	Diamond
CRYSTAL	Carnelian
ANIMAL	Ram
FOODS	Chile, onion, pepper, radish
PLANTS	Holly, nettle, poppy, thistle
TAROT CARD	The Emperor

THE WORLD OF TAURUS

CITIES	Dublin, Leipzig, Lucerne, Mantua
COUNTRIES	Eire, Iran, Russia, Switzerland, Zambia
COLOR	Green
NUMBER	Six
DAY OF THE WEEK	Friday
GEMSTONE	Emerald
CRYSTAL	Malachite
ANIMAL	Bull
FOODS	Apple, asparagus, wheat
PLANTS	Daisy, dandelion, violet
TAROT CARD	The Hierophant

THE WORLD OF GEMINI

CITIES	Cardiff, London, Melbourne, San Francisc
COUNTRIES	Barbados, Belgium, Sardinia, Wales
COLOR	Yellow
NUMBER	Five
DAY OF THE WEEK	Wednesday
GEMSTONE	Garnet
CRYSTAL	Agate
ANIMAL	Monkey
FOODS	Carrot, nuts
PLANTS	Buttercup, lavender, lily of the valley
TAROT CARD	The Magician

THE WORLD OF CANCER

CITIES	Amsterdam, Cadiz, New York, Tokyo
COUNTRIES	Africa, New Zealand, Scotland
COLORS	Mother-of-pearl, pearly gray, silver
NUMBER	Two
DAY OF THE WEEK	Monday
GEMSTONE	Pearl
CRYSTAL	Onyx
ANIMAL	Crab
FOODS	Cucumber, lettuce, milk, shellfish
PLANTS	Gardenia, lily, waterlily
TAROT CARD	The Chariot

_ACES AND THINGS RULED BY EACH ZODIAC SIGN

CITIES	Bristol, Chicago, Los Angeles, Rome
COUNTRIES	Italy (including Sicily), Romania
COLORS	Gold, orange
NUMBER	One
DAY OF THE WEEK	Sunday
GEMSTONE	Ruby
CRYSTAL	Rose quartz
ANIMALS	All members of the cat family
FOODS	Citrus fruits, honey, olives, rice
PLANTS	Camomile, daffodil, marigold, sunflower
TAROT CARD	Strength

CITIES	Bath, Boston, Jerusalem, Paris, Strasbourg
COUNTRIES	Brazil, Switzerland, Turkey, West Indies
COLORS	Dark brown, green, navy blue,
NUMBER	Five
DAY OF THE WEEK	Wednesday
GEMSTONE	Agate
CRYSTAL	Obsidian
ANIMALS	All domestic pets
FOODS	Barley, oats, root vegetables, rye
PLANTS	Buttercup, forget-me-not, speedwell
TAROT CARD	The Hermit

CITIES	Copenhagen, Frankfurt, Leeds, Vienna
COUNTRIES	Argentina, Austria, China, Japan, Tibet
COLORS	Pastel blues and pinks
NUMBER	Six
DAY OF THE WEEK	Friday
GEMSTONE	Sapphire
CRYSTAL	Jade
ANIMAL	Rabbit
FOODS	Asparagus, chocolate, grapes
PLANTS	Ash tree, hydrangea, violet
TAROT CARD	Justice

CITIES	Baltimore, Cincinnati, Dover, Liverpool
COUNTRIES	Algeria, Egypt, Morocco, Syria
COLOR	Dark red
NUMBER	Eight
DAY OF THE WEEK	Tuesday
GEMSTONE	Opal
CRYSTAL	Jasper
ANIMALS	Eagle, phoenix, scorpion
FOODS	Blackberry, garlic, onion
PLANTS	Hawthorn, heather, rhododendron
TAROT CARD	Death

PLACES AND THINGS RULED BY EACH ZODIAC SIG

THE WORLD OF SAGITTARIUS	
CITIES	Budapest, Cologne, Nottingham, York
COUNTRIES	Arabia, Australia, Hungary, Spain
COLOR	Purple
NUMBER	Three
DAY OF THE WEEK	Thursday
GEMSTONE	Amber
CRYSTAL	Turquoise
ANIMAL	Horse
FOODS	Celeriac, leek, onion,
PLANTS	Borage, carnation, dandelion, sage
TAROT CARD	Temperance

THE WORLD OF CAPRICORN	
CITIES	Brussels, Delhi, Frankfurt, Oxford
COUNTRIES	Albania, Bulgaria, India, Mexico
COLORS	Black, gray
NUMBER	Four
DAY OF THE WEEK	Saturday
GEMSTONE	Topaz
CRYSTAL	Lapis lazuli
ANIMAL	Goat
FOODS	Barley, meat, spinach
PLANTS	Ivy, pansy, yew tree
TAROT CARD	The Devil

THE WORLD OF AQUARIUS	
CITIES	Bremen, Hamburg, Salzburg, Stockholm
COUNTRIES	Canada, Ethiopia, Poland, Sweden
COLOR	Electric blue
NUMBER	Eleven
DAY OF THE WEEK	Saturday
GEMSTONE	Aquamarine
CRYSTAL	Peridot
ANIMAL	Bird
FOODS	Kiwi fruit, prickly pear, star fruit
PLANTS	Apple tree, orchid, Solomon's seal
TAROT CARD	The Star

THE WORLD OF PISCES	
CITIES	Alexandria, Seville, Warsaw
COUNTRIES	Egypt, Portugal, Scandinavia
COLORS	Sea green, turquoise
NUMBER	Nine
DAY OF THE WEEK	Thursday
GEMSTONE	Jasper
CRYSTAL	Chrysolite
ANIMAL	Fish
FOODS	Cucumber, pumpkin, watercress
PLANTS	Fig tree, waterlily, willow tree
TAROT CARD	The Moon

Aries

March 21–April 20

THE ARIES PERSONALITY

It's hard to ignore an Arien! It is natural for them to be leaders, not followers. The last thing any self-respectin Arien wants to do is simply to carry out other people's orders or be at their beck and call. They have to be in control of situations; they don't like it one bit when it's the other way round.

Being the first sign of the zodiac makes Ariens instinctively put themselves first. Even if their second thought concerns their nearest and dearest, their first thought will always revolve around themselves. There are degrees of this, of course. Occasionally, you may we meet a very selfish Arien who apparently doesn't realiz that anyone else in the world exists. These types are completely wrapped up in themselves and usually end up all alone. However, the vast majority of Ariens are merely slightly self-centered.

Life is very black and white for Ariens, with no half measures. That's partly because they belong to the Fire element, which gives them their infectious enthusiasm and adventurous spirit. The other reason is that this sign is ruled by the fiery planet Mars, making them short on temper and long on enthusiasm. They're very idealistic and always have high expectations that things will turn out well. As a result, they often do. Mar also gives them plenty of determination and a burning desire to achieve the things they set out to do. An Arien without a goal is a sad sight, because they feel lost without anything to aim for.

Ariens easily lose their temper but it's all over in a
ash. The only problem is the Arien bluntness—these
eople like to tell it how it is, and that can lead to hurt
elings when they go too far. Life would be much easier
r Ariens if they could curb their outspokenness. But
ien that would take so much fun out of things!

OVE

ove and romance are central to an Arien's life. But
ey also love the thrill of the chase, and some Ariens
id this is the most exciting part of any relationship.
iey cool off once they get what they want! The Arien's
enerous spirit and warm personality make them
wonderful friend and a delightful lover. Sex is very
iportant to them because it helps them to work off
eir abundant energy; they're demonstrative at the
est of times, and enjoy a very physical relationship
ith their lover. They won't be at all happy if their
irtner is not as passionate as they are.

Ariens have tremendous faith in other people. When
ey fall in love (which happens easily, probably more
ten than they care to admit), they invest everything
their lover. An Arien's partner holds their lover's fate
id happiness in their hands, and with luck nothing
ll go wrong. However, most Ariens have their hearts
attered at some point in their lives by someone who
ils to live up to their expectations.

Is this just one of those things or do Ariens somehow
ntribute to the situation? They certainly tend to

put loved ones on lofty pedestals. Everything's great while their loved one occupies this high position, but the moment they turn out to be human after all the Arien feels disappointed and crushed. If this person really causes the Arien a lot of pain, they'll never feel the same way about them again and it'll hurt like mac They find it very hard to learn from their mistakes.

CAREER

Ariens are free spirits, which means they can't abide any sort of job that ties them down or restricts their freedom. They need a job that gives them room to breathe otherwise they're likely to cause havoc by staging lots of rows with their boss or finding other ways to show their displeasure.

Something else that makes an Arien see red is having to account for their every action or carry out someone's instructions to the letter. If they're stuck in a job like this, they'll quickly become bored and frustrated, in which case they need interesting hobbie

The idea of being self-employed appeals to Ariens, who usually have a low opinion of their bosses and probably have one eye on their job. They're great at coming up with new ideas but will struggle to keep up the momentum the moment they hit a boring patch. Most Ariens find it hard to cope with donkey work.

Jobs connected with engineering, mechanics, the armed services, and sports, all appeal to Ariens. If they want to get to the top of their particular tree they're ɹite capable of doing so. They love coming first! ɪey're also excellent at dreaming up ideas, although .ey're not so hot at following them through—they are r happier if someone else does that for them!

ıONEY

ı Arien can't live without money! They love spending so an Arien can easily get carried away and part with r more money than they intended. They can't explain -it just happens!

Ariens also really enjoy spending money on ıything connected with transport, such as sports cars, :pensive motorbikes, or the latest mountain bike.

Something else that can drain an Arien's pockets their generosity. They can't bear the thought stinginess, so would rather end up broke than :cused of not paying their way. As a result they may ɪercompensate and buy loved ones all sorts of treats .at they can't really afford. High days and holidays ıd Ariens at their most vulnerable financially. Many them like to leave the present-buying until the last .inute, spending far more money than they intended.

Red is the Aries color and unfortunately their bank ılance often reflects this. They aren't interested in .ving money for the sake of it. If an Arien has some .oney in ther pocket, it gives them pleasure to spend it. ıey want to live for today, not tomorrow!

HEALTH

Ariens are blessed with lots of vitality and energy. If ar Arien can't get all this energy out of their system they soon start to feel restless, edgy, and irritable. That's when the fur can start to fly! Ideally, they should join their local gym or play plenty of sports. Their naturally competitive spirit means they're always determined t come first when playing against other people. Agree t play against an Arien at your peril, unless you've alrea observed them on the quiet and are pretty confident that you can beat them.

An Arien's natural shape is lean and muscular, so they hate the thought of gaining extra pounds. However, very often this happens as a result of their love of food and drink. It's important for them to take exercise in order to stay in peak condition.

Each sign rules a particular area of the body and Aries rules the head. As a result, members of this sign are especially susceptible to bumps on the head, and they may even have a couple of facial scars. Headache could be a problem but being active in the fresh air helps to blow away the cobwebs and keeps them feelir fit. Drinking plenty of water will also help to keep those headaches at bay and combat potential kidney problems, which are linked to Libra, the opposite sign Aries in the Zodiac.

OMPATIBILITY

ies with Aries

is can be too much of a good thing! When two Ariens t together there is always a lot of friendly (or not so endly) rivalry. They are always in competition with e another, even if it's tacit. They enjoy one another's mpany but can clearly see faults in the other that ey are blind to in themselves.

ies with Taurus

is is an awkward pairing. Aries and Taurus don't derstand one another. Ariens like to do things ickly while Taureans prefer to take their time. Even the Arien has much to teach the Taurean about ing spontaneous, and the Taurean can encourage e Arien to look before they leap. But they must be tient with one another.

ies with Gemini

iens and Geminis are on the same wavelength. ey thoroughly enjoy each other's company because ey share an enthusiasm for life and the desire to perience as much of it as possible. They're great ends, whatever the nature of their relationship. xually, however, the Arien may be too passionate and dent for the Gemini's liking.

Aries with Cancer

Sparks can fly with this couple because their needs are so different. The Arien is loyal but needs plenty of time to follow their own interests, and the Cancerian needs to feel they're loved and cherished 24 hours a day. Stalemate! They're better suited as friends than lovers when they'll run the risk of hurting one anothe without realizing it.

Aries with Leo

A good time is had by all when an Arien pairs up with a Leo. They both enjoy living it up, so it can be an expensive relationship. It's also a dramatic one, becau both signs are hot-blooded and impetuous. They have a good time sexually, and all is well provided the Arien doesn't have a roving eye!

Aries with Virgo

Plenty of tolerance is needed on both sides. The Arien likes to do things on the spur of the moment but this worries the Virgo who prefers to plan in advance. The Arien can also be too messy and untidy for the neat Virgo. They need to hit it off in the bedroom for this relationship to last.

ries with Libra

ıese two have plenty to learn from one another. The .plomatic Libran, who instinctively puts others first, ill learn to ask for what they want, while the self-entered Arien will learn to appreciate other people's eeds. Even so, plenty of give and take is needed, eferably not with the Libran doing all the giving and ıe Arien all the taking.

ries with Scorpio

ere are two people who share a passion for life. They ave enough in common to keep them interested . one another, but their very different sexual needs ay drive them apart. The Arien's easy-come-easy-go oproach to romance will make the intense Scorpio ıspect that they're just another notch on the bedpost.

ries with Sagittarius

ıis relationship is expensive but good fun! They enjoy ading each other astray, going to glitzy restaurants, ıd doing plenty of globetrotting. However, it will l fall apart very quickly if they don't laugh at each her's jokes! They get on very well sexually, provided erything stays light-hearted and easygoing.

Aries with Capricorn

It's a surprising combination but it works, provided the share the same ambitions. Both signs have a healthy respect for the good things in life and they'll work harc to get them. They also get on very well in the bedroom, because the Arien can encourage the Capricorn to forget their inhibitions and reveal their earthy side.

Aries with Aquarius

Friendship binds these two together. They're terrific mates no matter what their relationship. Emotionally however, they can hit problems if the Arien is very hot-blooded and passionate but the Aquarian is rather coc and detached. This will hurt the Arien and make them wonder what they're doing wrong.

Aries with Pisces

An Arien and a Piscean will struggle to maintain a sexual relationship for long. The Arien is too lusty and passionate for the sensitive Piscean, who will retreat emotionally, much to the Arien's bewilderment and hurt. However, they can be good friends, with the Arier encouraging the Piscean to loosen up and take a few risks every now and then.

Taurus

April 21—May 21

THE TAURUS PERSONALITY

People know Taureans are reliable, faithful, practical, and definitely people to turn to in a crisis. After all that it should come as no surprise that Taureans belong to the Earth element of the zodiac, making them responsible, steady, and trustworthy.

Taurus is one of the Fixed signs of the zodiac, which means that although Taureans are steadfast, they are also very resistant to the idea of change. A Taurean always takes a long time to get used to any major alterations in their life, and they can feel dislocated by the resulting change. As a result, a Taurean tends to slip into routines that quickly become ruts.

Some astrology books describe this sign as slow, but it would be fairer to say that Taureans take life at a measured pace. A Taurean can dash around when it suits them but a typical Taurean prefers to do things in their own time and in their own way—and will simply turn a deaf ear to anyone who tries to persuade them otherwise. In their favor, they have tremendous determination and willpower, but this can turn into a stubborn streak when the Taurean digs their heels in.

Being able to feed and clothe themselves is essential for any self-respecting Taurean. This means Taureans can accumulate a lot of belongings because, subconsciously, they see these as status symbols. They then become hemmed in by their possessions because they start to rule their lives—Taureans can't run the risk of losing all these objects that mean so much to them.

.s a result, they can't break out in new directions even ˙they want to because they're scared of what they ıight lose. Eventually, this can feel like a straitjacket, ut it may be too scary to do anything about it.

Of all the members of the zodiac, a Taurean is the ne least likely to lose their temper over trifles. The aurean will grit their teeth and give people the benefit f the doubt again and again, until things go too far. his can be a frightening experience for everyone ecause a Taurean really knows how to let rip! It's a ase of light the blue touchpaper and stand well back. Vhat's more, a Taurean can smolder for a long time fter the initial row has blown over and everyone else .as forgotten all about it.

.OVE

amily means the world to a Taurean, who will devote . lot of time to their nearest and dearest. Taureans eel comfortable around these people because they've nown them for such a long time and don't have to ıake much of an effort with them.

Taureans are loyal, loving, and steadfast. This ndears them to anyone who likes to know that their ffection won't be tossed away after the first, fine apture has waned. A Taurean makes a devoted friend nd they usually have a select circle of close long-time hums. It takes a Taurean quite some time to get o know people properly, and others have to earn a aurean's trust, but once they've done that the Taurean becomes the sort of pal who will stand resolutely by them through thick and thin.

Even though Taureans are very loving and affectionate, unfortunately this can sometimes turn into a tendency to be possessive. Sometimes a Taurean is so possessive that they hate to let their partner out of their sight and may object when other people lay claims on their time. If this possessiveness really starts to take root, the partner may run very fast in the opposite direction. Sadly, this may make the Taurean even more determined to cling on to the next person who they fall in love with. If a Taurean could only learn to let go and understand that the best way to keep someone's love is to give them their freedom, they would be much happier.

CAREER

Some signs don't like the thought of hard work but the Taurean doesn't mind it one bit. You can rely on a Taurean to get the job done. They may not polish it off as quickly as some of their fellow astrological signs, but at least they'll do it properly.

Self-employment isn't ideally suited to Taureans because they aren't happy with the thought of an irregular income and unpredictable working hours. However, they have plenty of discipline and motivation, so if a Taurean does decide to work for themselves they certainly won't fail through lack of trying. Their natural affinity with money means that any career connected vith finance, such as banking, insurance, consultancy, r investments, is right up their street.

Another suitable career is the beauty industry ecause a typical Taurean is a walking advert for beauty reparations. They make great models, beauticians, nasseurs, aromatherapists, and perfumiers. Taureans lso do well in professions connected with nature and he outdoors. There are many Taureans in the music ndustry too, especially singers, because this sign is lessed with beautiful voices.

MONEY

Money and Taurus go together like bread and butter. A Taurean understands money and respects it for what t can buy them. This can be summed up in one word -security. They will have sleepless nights if they think hey're going broke.

Their practical nature stands them in excellent tead when it comes to money matters and savings chemes appeal to the typical Taurean.

One of the first things Taureans like to do when hey've got some money is to buy a house of their own, oth as a nest-egg and to create a comfortable home. This will make them doubly happy!

It's important for every Taurean to make adequate inancial provision for the future, such as by investing n a solid pension and salting away any spare cash nto reliable savings accounts. It's another way for hem to bolster their physical and material security.

But this doesn't mean that most Taureans are miserly or tight-fisted—on the contrary, they can be the soul of generosity and enjoy sharing what they've got with their loved ones. Taureans also like treating themselves to luxuries, especially those that pamper them.

HEALTH

Each sign rules a particular part of the body. Taurus rules the throat—it may be their weak spot. When they feel run down, they can develop a sore throat or a stiff neck. They might also go quite hoarse, or possibly lose their voice altogether, in times of great emotion or stress.

Taureans enjoy taking life easy, and they also happen to enjoy a life-long love affair with food. Taureans put on weight quickly but find it difficult to lose it again, thanks to their slow metabolism. It's important for them to get plenty of fresh air and to combat the effects of what could be a sedentary job with lots of exercise. Something energetic like aerobics may not appeal, but they'll enjoy dancing or taking camping trips to explore the outdoors.

Being in the great outdoors is essential to a Taurean's well-being and happiness. Any Taurean who lives in a high-rise apartment will need to reconnect with nature, even if that means growing pot plants or tending a windowbox full of flowers or herbs. Gardening is a great way for Taureans to unwind. They also benefit from being able to walk barefoot through grass, which they find a very sensual experience.

ᴐMPATIBILITY

urus with Aries

'aurean struggles to work out what makes an Arien k. They like to adopt a practical approach to life iereas the Arien wants to take everything at a rush. ey can also feel short-changed emotionally, because e sort of smoldering passion they enjoy can make an .en feel uncomfortable and trapped.

urus with Taurus

hough this couple instinctively understand one other, that isn't always a good thing. They feel so e with each other that they can easily slip into a nfortable rut that excludes the rest of the world. The stinacy that they share can also mean there's no om for maneuver on the occasions when they fall out .h one another.

urus with Gemini

difficult to make this pairing work, especially .otionally. The Taurean is too passionate and earthy the light-hearted Gemini, who feels buried under an alanche of emotion. The Taurean will feel hurt if the mini devotes too much time to their independent :ial life. They're much happier as friends than lovers.

Taurus with Cancer

This is a pairing made in heaven! Both signs love thei home and family, and they share a strong need for emotional and material security. They'll revel in nest-building and cooking each other delicious but nourishing meals. Their sex life also keeps them smili because they have the same needs.

Taurus with Leo

The Taurean appreciates the Leo brand of loving, and the Leo adores being with someone so faithful. The main problem arises when they have arguments. The Leo wants to be the boss and dictate terms, but the Taurean will stand their ground and refuse to budge a inch. They must both learn to go with the flow.

Taurus with Virgo

This couple understand one another on many levels. The Taurean enjoys the Virgo's practical nature but won't appreciate being nagged about their dietary habits. The Taurean also likes peace and quiet, so ma have problems if the Virgo is very chatty. Emotionally the Taurean will teach the Virgo to be more open.

urus with Libra

th these people appreciate the finer things in life. ey also share a need for their relationships to be rmonious and easygoing. However, the dogmatic urean may lose patience if the Libran chooses to on the fence and rarely makes concrete decisions. od and drink play a large part in their relationship!

urus with Scorpio

ere's plenty of passion when these two get together. ey'll raise the temperature in the bedroom by eral degrees, enjoying a powerful sexual and otional rapport. They feel safe with one another cause they're both at heart faithful and loyal. The cid Taurean will help the Scorpio to tone down their ense approach to life.

urus with Sagittarius

hard for these two to stay together for long because y're poles apart. The Taurean is an instinctive ne-lover while the Sagittarian is a born traveler. sessiveness is bound to come between them, h the Taurean wanting—but failing—to hold on he Sagittarian and to temper their need for ependence.

Taurus with Capricorn

Both signs are too modest and conservative to admit it, but this is a very earthy and passionate combinatic They know where they stand with each other and tha they share the same down-to-earth approach to life. They also have a tacit agreement that the Taurean looks after the home and the Capricorn goes out and earns the money.

Taurus with Aquarius

This couple can't fathom one another out. The Taurea enjoys tradition and is shocked when the Aquarian dismisses this as sentimental twaddle. The loving Taurean is also easily hurt by the Aquarian's need to maintain some emotional distance. They feel threatened by the Aquarian's love of independence a wonder what it means.

Taurus with Pisces

This duo enjoy one another's company and are good friends. The Taurean feels protective toward the sensitive Piscean and enjoys taking care of them. The can also encourage the Piscean to be more practical and organized. All is well provided the straightforwar Taurean understands that their Piscean is a complicated being.

Gemini

May 22–June 21

THE GEMINI PERSONALITY

This is one of the most lively and vibrant signs of the zodiac. Geminis are mercurial, bright, and terrific company. Even better, they don't seem to age. Geminis love keeping up with the latest trends and their insatiable curiosity makes them as interested in knowing what their best friend is doing as in what's happening on the other side of the world.

The growth of the Internet and the entire technological revolution is a real gift to Geminis. Not only can Geminis continue to enjoy reading books, magazines, and newspapers, they can now chat to complete strangers. And as for cell phones . . . Well, chatterboxes like Geminis are in heaven!

It's certainly important for Geminis to keep in touch with people, and if they are on the Internet the probably email friends and family across the globe. They will gladly strike up a conversation with the pers standing behind them in the line at the supermarke or sitting next to them on the bus. Is this a polite way saying that Geminis love gossiping? Well, yes, actuall They love being first with the news.

It's all thanks to their planetary ruler, Mercury. He rules communications and the typical Gemini is a born communicator. Mercury is a liquid metal and Geminis also like to keep things fluid. In fact, Gemini can be really restless at times, unable to settle down anything or concentrate on one thing for long. If the aren't careful, this can lead to a superficial approach

Versatility is a Gemini's middle name and they can tainly tackle most things. A typical Gemini is also y adaptable, although sometimes this turns into ood swings and inconsistency. Geminis believe that ey operate on a steady, even keel but the people in eir life might not agree. Yes, a Gemini's emotions dip and down dramatically. A Gemini might think that's t the way they operate, but others call it moodiness. an also be hard to keep track of a Gemini's opinions cause they tend to change them often. A Gemini ctuates according to the circumstances and time day. It's all part of what makes a Gemini such an eresting person to have around.

)VE

e sign of Gemini belongs to the Air element, so minis are happiest when dealing with ideas. notions make them feel uncomfortable and it can hard for them to express their feelings. In fact, notions can make a Gemini embarrassed, tongue- d, and feel as though they've got two left feet. ey can also feel swamped by a partner who is very notional or prey to sudden rushs of feelings.

Because a Gemini has such a gift for words, they can scribe their emotions in an intellectual way but it is other story when it comes to experiencing and living eir feelings. Anyone who wears their heart on their eve makes a Gemini wince and want to rush off in e opposite direction.

There are problems when a Gemini is in a relationship with someone who's very clingy or possessive, because this is almost guaranteed to mak them do a rapid disappearing act. Unfortunately, som members of this sign are not exactly noted for their fidelity. Especially when young, they can enjoy playing partners off against one another or getting involved i some complex two-timing.

Even so, a Gemini's popularity rating is usually sky-high. People adore their sunny nature, their ready laugh, and their fascinating conversation. When looking for friends and lovers, a Gemini seeks out people who are on the same intellectual wavelength. No matter how devastatingly attractive someone is, Gemini won't stay with them for long if they're borin not very bright, or don't have a sense of humor.

CAREER

Communicating with others is second nature to Geminis. Most Geminis will find it a struggle to do anything that involves long periods of silence. They simply aren't cut out for a quiet life.

Geminis find it easy to get on well with their colleagues and clients—everyone warms to the Gemini's breezy personality and the Gemini enjoys getting to know their workmates as people in their ov right, not simply as colleagues.

A Gemini is an ideal candidate for any career in th media, communications industry, advertising, or sale

Gemini also needs a job with plenty of variation and, ieally, the chance to go traveling.

Because a Gemini finds it easy to do at least two nings at once, self-employment may also suit them. owever, they must cultivate the mental discipline to arry on working on those days when they'd rather tay in bed. Whatever their job, Geminis are completely lued up about the latest office gossip. They're the one ask if you want to know what's going on!

ONEY

Gemini can spend their cash as soon as they get it! ne area in which Geminis excel is in wheeling, dealing, nd negotiating. They could sell fish to penguins.

A big expense for many Geminis is keeping in touch ith the rest of the world. Many run up massive phone ills or buy the latest computer equipment. If they can fford it, they'll buy themselves all sorts of gadgets.

Finance doesn't mean much to them, yet they ertainly enjoy the things that money can buy. Finance itself might bore the typical Gemini to tears, but if ey turn it into an intellectual game they can become bsolutely fascinated. For instance, they will enjoy eading the business pages of newspapers in the same ay they read a gossip column—although the latest novements in their bank account might be a complete ystery to them.

They also enjoy impulse shopping, which can have a rastic effect on their bank balance.

HEALTH

A Gemini may give the impression of being game for anything and ready to stay up all night, but underneath it all they have a very sensitive nervous disposition. One of the easiest ways for a Gemini's system to go wrong is if they are bored. If they go through a period when their life becomes mundane and unexciting, it can make them feel quite ill. When this happens the Gemini needs to find positive outlets for their nervous energy, such as tennis—the perfect Gemini sport. A Gemini certainly likes it when life is busy and lively, although too many late nights will soon catch up with them. So will the typical Gemini diet of too much coffee and cigarettes and not enough solid food.

The average Gemini is no stranger to bouts of insomnia. Ideally, they should be active during the day so they crawl into bed dead tired.

Most signs fight the battle of the bulge, but many Geminis suffer from the opposite problem and find it difficult to gain weight. It's a problem that makes other signs go green with envy!

Gemini rules the arms, hands, and chest, so these are the most vulnerable areas of a Gemini's body. Typical Geminis gesticulate all the time so it's hardly surprising that occasionally these limbs make violent contact with something hard and the result is a bruise, strain, or even a fracture.

:OMPATIBILITY

;emini with Aries

hey really enjoy one another's company and share .n insatiable curiosity about the world. This is the sort f couple that always get each other into scrapes that hey laugh their way out of. Emotionally, the ardent and ery Arien can be hurt by the easygoing Gemini, who ometimes struggles to show their feelings.

;emini with Taurus

Vhat do these people see in each other? They're nuch better friends than lovers because they have uch different emotional needs. Also, the quick-witted ;emini soon loses their patience with the pragmatic aurean. The Gemini's ability to see at least two sides in .n argument flummoxes the straightforward Taurean.

;emini with Gemini

Vhen one Gemini pairs up with another, they're elieved to find someone who truly understands them. hey'll soon develop lots of in-jokes and will delight n trading puns and wisecracks. It will help if they are omfortable with showing their feelings, otherwise the elationship may become rather unemotional.

Gemini with Cancer

This is a super combination for business or friendship, but it isn't so hot for romance because these people are so different. At first, the Gemini enjoys the novelty value of being cherished by their Cancerian, but after a while they may start to feel suffocated and trapped. They're convinced there's more to life than home cooking.

Gemini with Leo

This fun-loving pair are made for each other. They share a terrific sense of humor and love teasing one another. The Gemini will gently bring the Leo down to earth when they get too full of themselves. The Gemini also revels in being the focus of the Leo's attention, although they may sometimes feel they can have too much of a good thing.

Gemini with Virgo

Put together two of the great communicators of the zodiac and what do you get? A lot of talk! This couple can chat right round the clock, always finding something new to discuss. However, such an emphasis on brainpower can hold them back emotionally, because neither of them is comfortable when talking about their feelings.

Gemini with Libra

his is one of the great combinations and both signs et a lot out of the relationship. They both look for lever partners so are secretly flattered that the other ne obviously rates them intellectually. They're good iends, lovers, or business partners. If anyone can ncourage a Gemini to express their softer and more omantic side, it's a Libran.

Gemini with Scorpio

his couple has virtually nothing in common yet they nake surprisingly good friends. Both of them are aturally curious and they're intrigued to know what nakes the other one tick. But it's a different story in sexual relationship, because the Gemini finds the corpio far too hot, heavy, and passionate for comfort.

Gemini with Sagittarius

hese people instinctively understand and complement ne another on many levels. They share a love of nental and physical exploration, so always have omething to talk about. They both have passing nthusiasms, although the Gemini may learn to go nto things in more depth after spending time with the nore reflective Sagittarian.

Gemini with Capricorn

It's the odd couple! All is well if the Capricorn has a dry sense of humor, but the Gemini will soon get fed up if they're with the sort of Capricorn who is morose and pessimistic. Even so, the Gemini can teach the Capricorn to lighten up, and can learn in return to take life a little more seriously. Sexually, it's either great or a complete disaster.

Gemini with Aquarius

Neither sign tolerates fools, so both individuals have to keep their brains up to the mark if they want the relationship to last. They enjoy getting involved in long discussions about whatever pops into their minds. Even if their relationship starts romantically, they will eventually become best friends, sometimes at the expense of their sex life.

Gemini with Pisces

They're good friends, although they occasionally have misunderstandings that upset the Piscean. However, they struggle to maintain a happy emotional relationship because there is so much scope for misunderstanding. The Gemini's glib remarks and sometimes cool emotions can quickly make the Piscean retreat in bewilderment.

Cancer

June 22–July 23

THE CANCER PERSONALITY

One of the most caring and sensitive signs in the zodiac, Cancerians are very popular with anyone who likes to feel cherished. It's partly thanks to the Moon, which rules the sign of Cancer, and partly to the fact that Cancerians belong to the Water element. Put those two things together and you get someone who is considerate, affectionate, and highly emotional.

The typical Cancerian loves being at home, because it's where they feel safest. A Cancerian may not even realize it, but they've probably filled their home with all sorts of precious mementoes and keepsakes that remind them of the past and of their loved ones. They may also have cupboards and drawers filled with all sorts of things that they no longer use but simply can't bear to throw away.

Cancer is the sign of the crab, and sure enough Cancerians tend to lead their lives in very crab-like ways. For instance, they often approach situations from an angle rather than directly. They have a tendency to manipulate people instead of making outright requests. They also tend to retreat into their shell whenever the going gets tough or they think they aren't appreciated.

Family life means everything to members of this sign. If a Cancerian doesn't get on well with their own kith and kin, or if they live very far away from them, they will compensate by creating a close-knit group of special friends. And these people consider themselves very lucky to be looked after by a Cancerian.

Because this is a Water sign, Cancerians often soak ɔ the atmosphere around them like a sponge. They ·e also very sensitive to other people's moods and in ·ne with their feelings. Some of them may even be ;ychic or have pronounced ESP abilities.

ƆVE

·en though a Cancerian is highly emotional, there is a ·ry shrewd side to them. It makes them a great judge character. However, their emotions often get in the ·ay of their judgment of people, making them either ·mpletely for or against them. Even if a Cancerian is ·vare of what's going on, it can be almost impossible r them to divorce themselves from their feelings.

The people in a Cancerian's life think of them as very fectionate, loving, and demonstrative. That's thanks their strong maternal instinct, which operates ·hether they're a man or a woman. If the Cancerian is ·nest, they'll admit that they can occasionally cling people too tightly and are reluctant to let them out their sight. This isn't because they want to control ·em, simply because they find it comforting being ·ound their loved ones.

A Cancerian can also struggle to allow a relationship come to the end of its natural life. They will pretend ·at nothing is wrong and try to keep the partnership ·ing for as long as possible.

A Cancerian is in clover when things are going well a relationship, but they can become awfully moody

and tense when they suspect that something's gone wrong. The bottom immediately falls out of their world. A Cancerian can become so defensive that they'll deliberately spark off a row, just so they can fire the first shot before the other person gets the chance to hurt them. If they can learn to relax more, their relationships will run much more smoothly and there will be fewer tears and less heartache.

CAREER

A typical Cancerian has a marvelous business brain, making them a natural candidate for a successful career. Cancerians know what they want from life and what's more, they know how to get it. A Cancerian is certainly not afraid of hard work, provided they're paid a decent wage and don't feel they are being exploited. Any job that involves looking after other people is idea for them, especially if they work in one of the caring professions or a service industry. They might enjoy being a nanny, nurse, or nursery teacher. Something else that would appeal is working in the antiques trad or as a silversmith.

The sign of Cancer has a strong affinity with histor so a Cancerian might enjoy being a historian, archivis or an archaeologist. They also have a fascination with photography. Many Cancerians are fantastic cooks, with an inbuilt understanding of what other people like to eat. A Cancerian might enjoy running their own bakery or restaurant.

Another possible string to a Cancerian's bow is omedy. Cancer is one of the signs that rule comedy ecause it places such importance on familiar things id we often laugh at jokes that strike a chord.

A Cancerian is much happier working with other eople than on their own, when they will soon become nely and depressed. However, they should try hard ot to absorb the atmosphere around them when ings get tense, because this will make them feel ill. ey need to cultivate a sense of detachment and self-eservation.

ONEY

nancially, Cancerians have got it taped! Cancerians ways have the upper hand financially, but only cause they value the things that money can buy id the happiness it can bring to their loved ones. For ample, one of a Cancerian's biggest priorities in life is live in a comfortable home, preferably owned rather an rented as they consider paying rent is a waste money. A Cancerian doesn't mind working hard to hieve this. Cancerians always enjoy spending money their loved ones. A typical Cancerian isn't a flashy ender and they buy items that are built to last.

Saving comes naturally to a Cancerian. They aren't terested in get-rich-quick schemes because they're ell aware of the risks involved. If a Cancerian is oking for interesting ways to invest their money, they ght be instinctively drawn to antiques and items

made from silver. That's because this is the metal ruled by Cancer, and because Cancerians have a strong affinity with things from the past.

HEALTH

Because their feelings are so central to a Cancerian's existence, every area of their life is bound to have an emotional impact on them. This can affect their healt and the results are usually stomach problems and digestive upsets, as well as an unpleasant, jittery feelir that doesn't want to go away. The best way to combat such ailments is for the Cancerian to learn to relax more, but that's a lot easier said than done because every Cancerian is a born worrier.

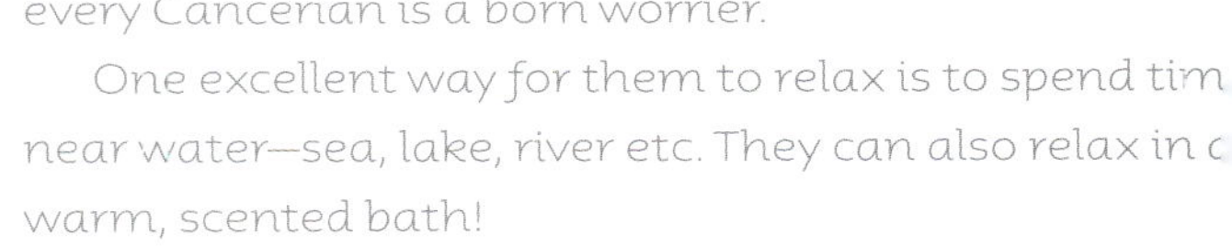

One excellent way for them to relax is to spend tim near water—sea, lake, river etc. They can also relax in a warm, scented bath!

Food—especially items that are high in calories and fat—is a great source of comfort to a Cancerian, especially when things are going wrong. Unfortunatel the effects of this are often more than obvious. Even s cooking is a wonderful form of therapy for them and, they are usually fantastic cooks, anyone they're cookir for will benefit as well.

As Cancerians get older they should make sure the get plenty of exercise to counter the effects of taking i too many calories. This will also give them something else to think about besides all those worries.

OMPATIBILITY

ıncer with Aries

s tough for these two to understand each other. ıe Cancerian way to anyone's heart is through their omach, and this works at first for the Arien who lores being the culinary center of attention. But it ılls after a while and the Cancerian needs to give their ien plenty of room to breathe and do their own thing. xually, though, it's hot stuff.

ıncer with Taurus

s a marriage made in heaven! Comfort, cosiness, ıd emotional safety are top priorities for both signs they've got it made when they get together. At st, the Cancerian has found someone who enjoys ing looked after and who shares their love of home mforts. The only problem is that they can get stuck in conservative rut.

.ncer with Gemini

.is is a strange mixture, especially in an emotional ationship. The Cancerian admires the way the emini rushes around doing several things at once, t can't match their hectic pace for long. They joy taking care of the Gemini but need to back off ery now and then, otherwise the Gemini can feel ıothered by too much attention.

Cancer with Cancer

When two homebodies pair up, it may take a miracle get them out of their own front door for longer than a trip to the shops. They will devote a lot of time and lov to making sure their home is as cosy and welcoming possible. They both need to talk about their feelings if they want to avoid long sulks and nasty silences wher things go wrong.

Cancer with Leo

Both signs place a big emphasis on the family, which immediately gives them a lot in common. They also enjoy looking after each other, ideally with the Leo wearing the trousers. Although they're both good at expressing their feelings, sometimes the Cancerian c retreat into sulks and silences which will soon get the Leo roaring with anger.

Cancer with Virgo

It's hard to know what these two see in each other. The Cancerian is a natural hoarder but the Virgo sees this as a way of collecting dust. All those rib-sticking Cancerian meals can also go unappreciated by the health-conscious Virgo. Emotionally, the Cancerian c feel short-changed by their no-nonsense Virgo.

ıncer with Libra

:spite their many differences, this couple really ›preciate one another. Neither of them likes conflict they'll work hard to maintain a harmonious :ationship. When problems arise, the Cancerian will lk about them and the Libran will brush them under e carpet. They will both find it hard to say goodbye if e relationship comes to an end.

ıncer with Scorpio

hat a happy couple! They share the same intense ıotional needs, although at times their private life n become as emotionally charged as a melodramatic era. There may be scenes and massive rows, but ey'll both enjoy making up afterward. Sexually, they .ve a very erotic and sensual time together.

ıncer with Sagittarius

:is is not a natural pairing because the Cancerian ı homemaker while the Sagittarian is a freer spirit ıo prefers to explore the world. Friendship between em is interesting because of their differences t any strong emotional contact will be fraught th difficulties. The Cancerian is easily hurt by the gittarian's blunt, no-nonsense style of honesty.

Cancer with Capricorn

If there's one person a Cancerian feels safe with, it's a Capricorn. They know they'll be looked after and that this person will treat them with respect. In return, they'll provide a happy home for the Capricorn. However, they wear their heart on their sleeve and it is easily damaged by the buttoned-down Capricorn.

Cancer with Aquarius

What do these two see in each other? The Cancerian doesn't know what to make of the wacky Aquarian, who may deliberately wind them up to see how they react. They will also be horrified when the Aquarian suggests breaking with hallowed traditions or says they've seen too much of the Cancerian's family. This relationship is hard work.

Cancer with Pisces

Here are two people who understand one another. They'll enjoy taking care of each other and can happily share their feelings. However, they aren't so good at talking about any problems between them. A favorite pastime is watching tear-jerker films and indulging in orgies of weeping. They'll have a lovely time!

Leo

July 24—August 23

THE LEO PERSONALITY

This is the most regal sign of the zodiac. Every Leo worth their salt has an air of dignity and they behave accordingly. It's as if Leos know they're different from everyone else and don't want us to forget it. That's because Leos are ruled by the Sun which is, after all, th center of our solar system and literally the light of our lives. We would die without the Sun and, on some level Leos know that everyone else would wither up without them. Leos are life enhancing!

If you're trying to spot a Leo, look at their hair first. Most Leos have luxuriant, thick manes, and always tak a lot of trouble over them. Their hair is one of the first things you'll notice about them.

Leo belongs to the Fire element, which makes members of this sign exuberant and enthusiastic, as well as very warm and affectionate. Everyone needs at least one Leo in their lives, simply for the ego boosts they'll receive from their Leo friend. Leos don't suffer fools gladly—as a Leo friend you'll have passed the acid test and been accepted into their inner circle.

Occasionally Leos can be snobby and far too full of themselves. Luckily, however, these are the exception that proves the rule. Most Leos are quietly confident and don't feel the need to prove how great they are. Al the same, it's very important for a Leo to feel they've made an impression on people, but this generally happens quite naturally—a Leo doesn't have to put on airs and graces to do it.

Family matters are very dear to every Leo's heart. ney place a lot of importance on keeping in touch with cattered members of the clan. They also like gathering neir relatives around them every now and then.

Leo is the sign of creativity, and any Leo who can't xpress their talents in one way or another will soon ecome frustrated and irritable. Of course, creativity omes in many forms, but key Leo activities include ancing, acting, and painting. They also enjoy ppreciating other people's artistic abilities, especially the cinema and theater. This is the sign of drama!

OVE

ove and Leo go together. The sign of Leo rules the eart and Leos find it very easy to show affection to ne people in their lives. Once someone has captured Leo's affections, they'll always retain a place in the eo's heart unless they hurt them so deeply that they an never forgive them. For a sign with such a dignified, tately reputation, a Leo is surprisingly vulnerable nderneath that confident exterior. The Leo's pride nakes them reluctant to reveal that they've been hurt, lthough when things get really bad they'll make a big ong and dance about it, roaring their objections and eing full of righteous indignation.

Loyalty comes high on a Leo's list of emotional riorities—they are extremely faithful and expect their over to behave in the same way. Because this is a Fire ign, it's second nature for a Leo to show their affection with plenty of hugs and kisses. Sex is also an importan way for a Leo to demonstrate their expansive affections. If a Leo is denied these all-important outlet they find other ways of expressing their emotions. Their friends can look forward to being cherished and made a big fuss of! There's only one small snag in relationships, and that's the Leo's tendency to boss other people about. It's not that the Leo means to do it more that they simply can't help themselves!

CAREER

A Leo has tremendous potential and can turn their hand to virtually anything. A typical Leo adores stretching themselves by discovering fresh talents and skills, and they are also blessed with plenty of creative and artistic ability. It's a matter of pride for a Leo to know they're putting everything into their work, so the will feel let down and cheated if their job fails to live up to their expectations or they suspect they're wasting their time. A Leo needs to be emotionally involved with their work, and anything less than that simply won't do. It will upset them if their efforts go unnoticed by their boss or colleagues.

Leos excel at anything involving organization—if a Leo can't make things happen, no one can. A Leo will derive enormous satisfaction from setting up systems and making sure that everyone does what's expected c them. Sometimes, however, the people who work with them will accuse them of being bossy and demanding.

Leos need to take center-stage in some way. It's a are Leo who's content to work on the sidelines or to let omeone else enjoy the limelight. That's why so many eos work in the entertainment industry as actors, ancers, singers, and designers. Leos also enjoy using heir many creative and artistic talents in other ways, uch as painting, fashion, sport, and cooking.

ONEY

eos need money because they have certain standards hat they like to maintain. Only the best is good nough for a Leo! As a result, their finances may be ermanently stretched to the limit. A Leo's idea of eaven is to go into the most expensive shop they an find and then buy up as many luxuries as possible. uality not quantity is their motto.

Loved ones benefit from the innate Leo generosity ecause a Leo adores lavishing presents on them, just o let them know they care. It gives a Leo tremendous elight to spoil their favorite people, no matter how nuch it costs them.

The Leo needs to put some money away for the uture, so they've got something to draw on if times re hard or they need cheering up. Despite being an nthusiastic Fire sign, a Leo likes to stick to traditional ays of saving money. If they're looking for an nteresting investment they could be attracted to xpensive jewelry or objects made of gold—that way, ney can enjoy wearing their nest-egg.

HEALTH

It won't come as a surprise to hear that a Leo's love of the good life can have a dramatic effect on their waistline. Unless a Leo takes a lot of exercise, it's easy for them to put on weight and very hard for them to shift it again. This is something that every self-respecting Leo loathes because they always like to look their very best. Although exercise is important for every sign, it's essential for Leos because without it they can become very sluggish and irritable.

Two areas of the body are ruled by Leo—the heart and the back. A Leo therefore needs to keep their heart healthy by avoiding too many fatty foods and making sure they keep fit. They should look after their vulnerable back by investing in well-made chairs and a good-quality bed. It will also help if they can learn how to lift objects properly without the risk of damaging their delicate lumbar region.

If the thought of working out in a gym makes a Leo so exhausted that they want to lie down, they should try to combine taking exercise with something sociable. They could join a sports club that has excellent social facilities so that they can enjoy themselves with friends. Dancing is perfect for Leos, because it allows them to express their considerable creative talents.

COMPATIBILITY

eo with Aries

here's much excitement with this pairing. Both like o throw themselves into life and egg each other on o further exploits. The Leo's dignity can sometimes e shaken by the Arien tendency to blurt out their houghts, but their sense of humor will see them hrough. Sexually, sparks can fly!

eo with Taurus

verything will go swimmingly with this couple until hey fail to see eye to eye. When this happens, hell could reeze over before either of them is prepared to back lown or say sorry. They need to find ways around this ixity to reach a compromise. The Leo values loyalty and njoys knowing that their Taurean will stand by them hrough thick and thin.

eo with Gemini

his couple really know how to have fun. They nstinctively like each other and get on well in both latonic and passionate relationships. The Leo enjoys he Gemini's bubbly personality but can sometimes eel frustrated by their apparent inability to stop joking round and talk about their deepest feelings. They hould encourage the Gemini to unwind.

Leo with Cancer

This pair have a lot going for them. They're both family-minded and so enjoy gathering their kith and kin around them. The Leo will greatly enjoy using their brilliant organizational skills on their sometimes chaotic Cancerian. The Leo will also excel at comforting the Cancerian when life gets them down, but won't want to mop up the tears too often.

Leo with Leo

The big question is which one of them will be boss? When two Leos get together, power struggles are bound to erupt sooner or later. Ideally, they should mark out different areas of territory so they both rule the roost at times. Emotionally and sexually, they're hot stuff. Financially, this could be a very expensive combination

Leo with Virgo

This isn't the easiest combination in the world. The enthusiastic Leo will soon become irritated by the Virgo's pedantic need to nail down details, and frustrated by their reluctance to act on the spur of the moment. There may also be clashes over expenditure, with the Leo wanting to splash out while the Virgo prefers to count the pennies.

eo with Libra

ere we have the two signs for whom love makes ne world go round. They get on like a house on fire, lthough sometimes the Leo will be irritated by the bran's inability to make up their mind. Romantically nd sexually, however, they're in heaven. They're terrific iends, perfect lovers and good business partners.

eo with Scorpio

nis is a powerful combination, provided the Leo is repared to be swept along by the Scorpio's intense ttitude to life. There can be no half-measures with is relationship—the Scorpio simply won't allow it. This ould be the greatest sexual passion the Leo has ever ncountered but they'll balk at the Scorpio's tendency be suspicious and jealous.

eo with Sagittarius

nese two spur one another on to all sorts of dventures. They're enthusiastic about life and enjoy pending money, so it could be an expensive pairing, pecially when it comes to travel. The sky's the limit ith these two! The Leo will enjoy the Sagittarian's nse of humor but may feel they aren't always treated ith the respect they think they deserve.

Leo with Capricorn

Outward impressions are everything for these two. They share the need to cut a dash and command respect, so they'll work hard to create the image of the perfect couple. But it may be different behind the scenes, with the Leo sometimes feeling sidelined by the Capricorn's workaholic tendencies and their emotional reserve.

Leo with Aquarius

These people are fascinated by each other. They're very different yet they secretly admire one another for those very differences. They have plenty to talk about but the Leo can feel neglected emotionally if the Aquarian finds it hard to show their feelings or be physically demonstrative. Even if they break up, they'll probably stay friends.

Leo with Pisces

This is a strange pairing. Although both signs are very affectionate and loving, that's just about all they have in common. Is it enough to hold them together? Only if the Leo has the patience to weather all those Piscean storms of emotion and doesn't tear their hair out when their Piscean's life descends into total chaos yet again

Virgo

August 24—September 23

THE VIRGO PERSONALITY

It's tough being a Virgo. Virgos seem to attract a heap criticism. Even when a Virgo tells you their astrological sign they'll often add apologetically that they know how boring they are. But is this fair?

For instance, Virgos are perfectionists. Unfortunately, sometimes this means they can't leave something alone and will fiddle with it endlessly. When they wake up in the middle of the night, their first thought may be that they forgot to do something during the day.

But when you want something done, to whom do you turn? The person who couldn't really care less whether they do the job properly, or the person who w stick at it until they're happy with the results? In other words, given the chance you'd choose a Virgo every time. We all would.

Virgo is the second sign of the Earth element, whic means that a Virgo takes a very practical approach to life. This makes them wonderfully methodical, efficien and sensible. People rely on them but may also take them for granted.

Virgos are famous for their modesty, but this can lec to lack of self-confidence. A Virgo's opinion of themsel is often much lower than everyone else's because they're so aware of what they see as their failings. The are the sorts of faults that everyone suffers from, b the Virgo will view them as major character flaws. Why can't they be tidier, neater, more organized ...

eedless to say, no one else would recognize the irgo from their own character assessment.

Another very Virgoan characteristic is being critical. irgos have very high standards and apply these gorously. As a result, they can sound rather harsh and nsympathetic at times. When you're on the receiving nd of this sort of treatment, it may help to remind ourself that the Virgo is even tougher on themselves

Virgos dislike drawing attention to themselves. They ay choose classic clothes in conservative colors rather an the latest fashion. They like to look well turned out nd will rarely look messy.

OVE

s very hard for them to show their emotions, perhaps ecause this reveals the vulnerable side of their rsonality that they're always at pains to cover up. is can cause misunderstandings with loved ones. is is when their most unattractive trait comes to e surface—their tendency to carp and criticize. This rt of behavior can definitely drive a wedge between Virgo and their loved ones, because no one likes ing continually weighed in the balance and found nting. If this is a problem for a Virgo, they should encouraged to relax more and to think before they eak. They should also ask themselves why it's so portant for things to be done perfectly.

Virgos are much more brainy than their fellow Earth ns, Taurus and Capricorn. They need a partner who

will share their need to talk things through. This is not a sign that suffers fools gladly so they will soon lose patience with anyone who has fluff for brains.

Despite their modest and polite appearance, a Virgo can be pretty hot stuff in the bedroom. They enjoy casting aside that reserved demeanor! But they can become tongue-tied when it comes to saying how they feel. They can even find it difficult to be verbally demonstrative with friends, so need someone who will encourage them to open up more.

CAREER

We all rely on Virgos. They're so practical and efficient that they excel at making sure offices, businesses, and organizations are ticking over. Virgos are brilliant at creating filing systems and other arrangements that make everything run like clockwork.

Speaking of clockwork, most Virgos are very good timekeepers. They don't like to be kept waiting by others and so they take pride in making sure they're o time. As far as they're concerned, time is money. They feel uncomfortable if they have to spend too long in th spotlight, but they thrive on being a valued member o a support team or advisory committee.

Among the professions that are right up a Virgo's street are being an agent, accountant, secretary, teacher, writer, critic, scientist, doctor, or nurse. A Virgo has a very enquiring mind, so needs a job that stretches their brain. They'll hate any job that bores o

ultifies them, or which doesn't make the most of their
emendous potential.

Although some Virgos are self-employed, most of
iem prefer the structure of working with other people.
iey also like the security of knowing they'll receive
gular salary payments.

IONEY

ie combination of the Virgo's Earth element and
eir intelligent planetary ruler, Mercury, makes them
formidable number-cruncher. They like to keep track
where they stand financially. It's not that Virgos are
iserly; they just don't like wasting money. A typical
rgo has a good eye for a bargain and doesn't feel
ppy about splashing out on frivolous luxuries or
tle treats—they rarely believe that they deserve such
pperies. The people you see in supermarkets tapping
ımbers into their calculators in order to compare the
lue of similar items are probably Virgos!

When a Virgo needs to spend money on anything
ıportant or expensive, they won't jump into it on a
ıim. They will probably also do a lot of research to
ake sure they buy the right model and will question
e salesperson at length—woe betide them if they
n't have all the answers at their fingertips!

If a Virgo wants to invest some money, they'll be
ppiest if they can seek some sound financial advice
st. They will prefer to know that their capital is
owing steadily rather than in volatile fits and starts.

HEALTH

Every sign has a favorite hobby, and health is a big preoccupation for many Virgos. At best, a Virgo is very interested in staying healthy and is always keen to ensure they're eating the best possible diet and are getting plenty of exercise. At worst, they're a bit of a hypochondriac whose favorite bedtime reading is a medical encyclopedia—then they can lie awake all night worrying about all the ailments for which they obviously have the symptoms.

Stress and anxiety are definitely among the bigges health challenges for a Virgo. Once a Virgo starts to fret, their sensitive digestive system (which is ruled by this sign) begins to get snarled up, leading to stomach upsets, constipation, and irritable bowels. And it's vital important that a Virgo learns to relax! Meditation car be very good for them because it encourages them to observe themselves and sit still—many Virgos spend lots of time dashing hither and thither, with barely a moment to sit down for a meal.

Virgos very often benefit from a wholefood, organi or vegetarian diet. Not only does this help their vulnerable digestion to work more efficiently, it also makes them feel much more energetic and less tired.

OMPATIBILITY

irgo with Aries

nis is one of the most difficult pairings of all. They're different and want such different things out of life! ne painstaking Virgo despairs of the impulsive Arien, ho often seems to leap from crisis to crisis with great nthusiasm. They also find their lusty and passionate rien too hot to handle for long.

irgo with Taurus

nere's a strong rapport between these two. It may not e the sort of relationship that will set the world alight ut they both enjoy the comfortable predictability it. They both know where they stand, which is important to them. Some of the sexual games uggested by the naughty Virgo will shock the rather aid Taurean but they'll play along!

irgo with Gemini

nis is a meeting of minds. In some respects they're ery different and in others they have a lot in common, hich gives them plenty to talk about. They're more omfortable as friends or business partners than they e as lovers, because their contrasting emotional yles can lead to misunderstandings and pain.

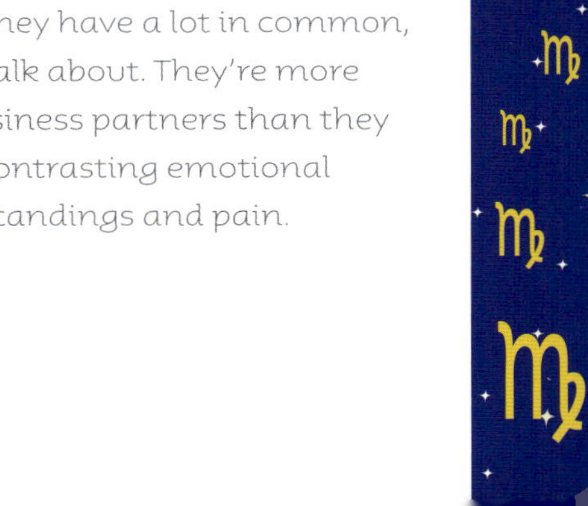

Virgo with Cancer

There's a lot to be said for this combination, although it often works best as friends rather than partners. The Virgo appreciates the caring qualities of their Cancerian but can sometimes feel as though they're losing their independence. They also struggle to meet the Cancerian's powerful emotional needs because they simply don't understand them.

Virgo with Leo

This is a difficult combination. The naturally modest Virgo is often baffled and even slightly shocked by the Leo's leanings toward conspicuous consumption and possibly even outright swank. They also find it hard to tolerate the way their Leo dramatizes situations. It's all too much for the practical and sensible Virgo to tolerate for long.

Virgo with Virgo

Although no one understands a Virgo like another Virgo, this can be a rather tepid combination. Ideally, one, if not both, of the Virgos needs to be much more emotional than usual to prevent the relationship from becoming mired in reservations and modesty. They can talk all they want, but need to find an emotional meeting ground as well.

irgo with Libra

hese two are much happier as friends than lovers ecause this helps to prevent bad feelings and hurt. The ver practical Virgo can help the Libran to get their life ogether and will encourage them to reach decisions. irgo enjoys the Libran's intellectual abilities but can ecome suspicious of their charm and diplomacy. Are ney really that nice?, they wonder.

irgo with Scorpio

here's an endless fascination between these two signs. hey both enjoy analyzing what makes other people ck and they have plenty of scope putting each other's ascinating foibles under the microscope. The trouble an start if they allow their relationship to become o analytical and they forget about expressing their eelings. Sexually, it's dynamite!

irgo with Sagittarius

ere's a tricky one. They enjoy talking and admire one nother's brainpower, but the Virgo will quickly become nnoyed by the Sagittarian's apparent inability to tick to the facts. They'll correct their Sagittarian every me they start to exaggerate and an undercurrent of riction will soon drive a wedge between them. They're etter friends than lovers.

Virgo with Capricorn

These people understand one another. They share the need for an ordered life that runs as smoothly as possible. So what if it's slightly boring—at least it feels safe. The Virgo heartily admires the Capricorn's respect for the power of money and they also approve of the Capricorn's ability to be a workhorse. In the bedroom, they're surprisingly hot stuff.

Virgo with Aquarius

Both these people have very strong opinions and they're eager to tell one another all about them. They fare much better as friends than as lovers, because then their long conversations won't get in the way of the action. If they are lovers, the Virgo will soon feel frustrated by the Aquarian's apparently take-it-or-leave-it attitude to sex.

Virgo with Pisces

This is a difficult combination. The Virgo prides themself on being pragmatic and sensible, so is driven to distraction by the Piscean's chaotic way of life. They also quickly lose patience if the Piscean apparently lurches erratically from crisis to crisis. The Virgo's suggestions of ways to improve things are seen by the Piscean as implied criticism.

Libra

September 24—October 22

THE LIBRA PERSONALITY

When you meet a Libran for the first time, your overriding impression will be of someone who is charming, diplomatic, and eager to put you at your ease.

Harmony is very important for members of this sign. They can't bear it when tempers are frayed or the atmosphere is tense. This sign is symbolized by the scales, and all Librans strive to create balance in their lives. But this doesn't mean their scales are always level. Instead, they fluctuate wildly up and down, with the Libran desperately trying to control the situation. They like to find a happy medium and to strike the right note at difficult moments.

It's very calming and relaxing to be around a Libran, even if they're a knot of tension inside. Part of this is thanks to their ability to put other people first and themselves second. You feel that they truly appreciate your company. However, you may be surprised to see them treating everyone else in the same way!

Librans can thank their planetary ruler, Venus, for their megadose of charm. Venus ensures they rarely put a foot wrong. Tradition says that Libra is one of the best looking signs in the zodiac—an accolade shared with Taurus. They have instinctive good taste and as they get older they prefer classic clothes to the latest fashion.

Although Librans have a reputation for being charm on legs, there's quite a tough side to them. Some astrologers say that a Libran is really an Arien on their best behavior. For instance, forget the idea that a Libra ever loses their temper. It's healthy for them to let off team and the eruption is usually far less tempestuous they allow themselves frequent outbursts. They are lso good at being grumpy, subtly implying that if only ou had behaved differently they wouldn't have to be so nnoyed with you.

Libra is one of the three Air signs, which means they re happiest operating on an intellectual level. The ombination of peace-loving Venus, who makes them eluctant to hurt people, and their brainy element of ir, means they always see at least two sides to every tory and tend to sit on the fence. Is it any wonder that ney're known for their indecision?

OVE

his is one area of life where Librans do really well. The ign of Libra rules partnerships of all kinds, including pen enmity. In fact, Librans can feel like a fish out of vater if they have to spend too long on their own. Their eady charm ensures their popularity and they can be xtremely affectionate, loving, and romantic. People nd it hard to resist them!

A Libran is much happier in a relationship than out f one. This means they prefer to stay in a dead-end elationship rather than risk being left on the shelf. Very ften, it's a Libran's partner who instigates the break.

It's very easy for other people to hurt a Libran's eelings, although they'll do their best to put on a brave ace. Romance is the Libran's Achilles heel and it can break a Libran's heart over and over again. They are also very idealistic and will turn a blind eye to their partner's faults. When they do find a special someone, they tend to put them on a pedestal, looking up to them and inevitably feeling crushed and disappointed when this person reveals that they're human after all. Sadly, there are times when someone hurts a Libran but they come straight back for more—it's as if they can't learn from the experience.

CAREER

A typical Libran enjoys the high life. As a result, unless they have been left a fortune, they need a good job tha brings in lots of cash.

Pleasant surroundings are very important to a Libran. It's also important for them to feel happy with their colleagues, because they'll hate coming into work if there's a tense atmosphere. Librans can't bear nit-pickers or troublemakers.

Even so, don't make the mistake of thinking that a Libran is a pushover at work. They can be surprisingly tough when the stakes are high enough and are capable of driving a hard deal.

In a perfect world, a Libran should be part of a team because they can find it difficult to motivate themselve sometimes when doing an unpleasant task. They are also not very good at keeping track of systems and being organized, because they tend to postpone anything tedious or difficult for another day.

Any job that makes the most of a Libran's charm ıd intellect will bring out the best in them, for stance diplomacy, fashion, beauty, and music.

ONEY

ıis is a very important part of a Libran's life because orans have got to pay for all the luxuries that they ve. There are so many things to spend money on, at their biggest worry is deciding what to buy first. e arrival of their second worry usually coincides with e appearance of their bank statement. And it's not lped by their inbuilt reluctance to confront anything pleasant or ugly, so they'll tell themselves that things e a lot better than they imagine.

However, it's essential that the Libran avoids any ndency to lavish gifts on people and their loved ones cause they want to buy their affection, rather than cause they want to make them happy.

Occasionally you will meet a Libran who uses a mbination of charm and cash to get what they want. ot only does this cause resentment in the person ıo is being bought, the Libran is probably fooling emselves about their motives, telling themselves that ey're being generous out of the goodness of their art. When this is thrown back in their face, they'll be l of righteous indignation. It is far better for a Libran be honest about what they want, and to trust that ople will love them for themselves rather than their ending power.

HEALTH

Librans are very healthy on the whole. However, their enjoyment of the good life means that they have a tendency to put on weight. It's one of the disadvantag of being ruled by Venus—this planet bestows good looks, immense charm, and a beautiful voice, but also makes its subjects prone to piling on the pounds. Minc you, the fact that most Librans have a sweet tooth an enjoy eating rich foods won't help much either. The best antidote to this is plenty of exercise but, unless the Libran is very unusual, the thought of this doesn't exactly make them want to put down that doughnut, leap off the sofa and put on their jogging kit. They nee a little encouragement.

Everyone benefits from some form of exercise, so the Libran should try to find a sport or activity that tru appeals to them, otherwise they'll never stick with it. Another secret to success is to make sure they exercis regularly and steadily.

The area of the body ruled by Libra is the kidneys, s Librans need to keep an eye on any irregularities that are indicated by inexplicable headaches or backache. If their social life involves drinking a lot of alcohol, the should try to combat its effects with plenty of water a fruit juices to flush out all those toxins.

OMPATIBILITY

ra with Aries

hen this couple first get together, they're intrigued by e another. Later on, however, the Libran is shocked the Arien's self-centered attitude and the hot-aded way they lose their temper. Sexually, it can all come a bit too much for the gentle Libran if the Arien s an insatiable libido. The Libran may end up feeling le better than a sex object.

ra with Taurus

is couple believe in enjoying themselves so they'll sh the boat out at every opportunity. Their shared e of beauty brings them together, but the Libran will d it hard to cope if the Taurean is possessive or wants ery restrictive relationship. They may also clash over eir differing intellectual needs.

ra with Gemini

re are two people who can really have a lot of together. The Libran appreciates the Gemini's ely mind and quick wit, and is delighted to be with meone who shares their high level of brainpower. ven time, they can encourage the Gemini to be ore emotional and demonstrative, and to feel less barrassed about revealing their softer side.

Libra with Cancer

Both these people want to be happy. However, they can have differing views on what this means, with the Libran wanting peace at all costs and the Cancerian valuing family life above all else. The Libran might enjo being with the Cancerian's family but will soon decide that they can have too much of a good thing.

Libra with Leo

This is a show-stopping relationship. It can also have a pretty dramatic effect on the couple's finances, because neither sign likes to stint themselves. They'll egg each other on to enjoy the best that money can buy. Emotionally, they bring out the best in one anoth although the Libran may find that the Leo appears over-dramatic at times.

Libra with Virgo

Friendship is a much better bet than love for this couple. The Libran enjoys having the Virgo as a friend, and will benefit from their no-nonsense attitude. However, as a lover the Libran will feel perplexed and rather hurt by the Virgo's slightly remote attitude. The have such different approaches to life that it's difficult to find any middle ground.

›ra with Libra

last the Libran has found someone who truly ›preciates them! They enjoy taking care of one ıother and will spend many happy hours shopping, :ting, and generally having as good a time as possible. won't take much for them to live beyond their means ıt they won't really care because it's all so much fun.

›ra with Scorpio

.is is a difficult pairing because they simply don't ıderstand one another. Although the Libran could ırn a lot from the Scorpio's ability to immerse emselves in their emotions, they can't bear the ›ought of losing control like that. The Scorpio's ssionate approach to sex can also be too strong for e Libran to tolerate.

›ra with Sagittarius

pect plenty of laughs and infectious high spirits ıen these two get together. The Libran enjoys the gittarian's natural optimism, enthusiasm, and od humor, and also likes being with someone ıo's a match for them intellectually. They'll spend any happy hours talking about all sorts of subjects. ıotionally, they have a good rapport.

Libra with Capricorn

This is a good business partnership, provided the Libran is prepared to match the Capricorn's round-the clock working pattern. However, it can be an uneasy emotional relationship because the Libran is often disconcerted by the Capricorn's rather distant and reserved attitude. They can misconstrue this emotion coolness as lack of interest.

Libra with Aquarius

What a great combination! This couple enjoy one another's company and really benefit from being together. The Libran may even learn to be more decisive, thanks to the Aquarian's cut-and-dried opinions. Intellectually, this is a marvelous match. Emotionally, it's got a lot going for it, provided the Aquarian is happy to show their feelings.

Libra with Pisces

These are the two great romantics of the zodiac, so yo can expect plenty of hearts and flowers. They have a l in common, both preferring to ignore anything nasty in life. However, this can cause problems if it means they both turn a blind eye to the difficulties in their relationship. They should encourage each other to be more realistic and clear sighted.

em to examine situations in depth is ideal for them, they could be attracted to detective work, the law, ience, medicine, research, mining, or the wine trade.

ONEY

eryone needs money to survive, but Scorpios need it ore than most. Financial security is very important them because of the power and independence it ves them. They may enjoy knowing that they've got ore money than their friends, or they may get great tisfaction from knowing that money enables them to e comfortably. If they have enough money, they try to ve some of it to a good cause.

Sometimes, a Scorpio will try to use money to buy wer and control over other people. They will probably this in a very subtle way and may not even be nscious of what they're doing. But they will place a of importance on status symbols and appearances. ey may also mortgage themselves up to the hilt in der to live in the sort of house that their family and ends can only dream of.

If they have any cash to spare, a Scorpio likes the ought of investing it in stocks and shares. They e being linked with some of the world's biggest mpanies. They are canny investors and will enjoy aying the stock market. However, if they want to sleep undly at night they should try not to put all their eggs one basket or invest more money than they can ford to lose.

HEALTH

Because they tend to concentrate their energies and channel them in particular directions to the exclusion of all else, a Scorpio must make sure they don't becom blocked or frustrated in any way. If they do, they could feel the effects physically, through strange illnesses or a deep sense of frustration. They may also suffer from problems with their genitals, parts of the body which are ruled by Scorpio.

'Moderation in all things' is a good Scorpio motto, but whether members of this sign follow it is quite another matter. It's all or nothing for Scorpios. As a result, they mustn't overdo it when they take exercise They should try to release their energies smoothly and steadily, and not alternate long periods of inactivity with protracted bouts of intense exercise.

This tendency to go overboard also extends to food and drink. This means they can sometimes feel wretched due to excessive alcohol consumption and a crushing hangover or after eating too much rich food Their sensitive digestive system is usually affected, causing constipation or an upset stomach.

If a Scorpio does decide to take some more exercis they could try something that encourages them to move in a controlled yet powerful way, such as t'ai chi, yoga, or one of the martial arts. It's easy for a Scorpio to bottle up problems, so if they choose an activity tha also helps them to relax, so much the better.

OMPATIBILITY

:orpio with Aries

ıere's plenty of heat and passion here. But the Scorpio ɛes to play their cards close to their chest and may ıd the Arien rather too direct and forthright for their ıste. Sexually, lots of sparks will fly—and not only notionally. The Scorpio likes to be seduced but the ·ien sometimes doesn't have time for such niceties.

:orpio with Taurus

ıis is a happy couple! They have plenty in common but ıough differences to keep life interesting. The Scorpio always relieved when they know where they stand ıd this is more than likely with a straightforward, loyal .urean. They both enjoy their home comforts and will ıppily create a cosy nest they can retreat to.

:orpio with Gemini

ıis can be a mismatch. They have such contrasting ıys of looking at life that they'll have to work hard make their relationship a success. The Scorpio may frustrated by the Gemini's apparently superficial titude and may also suspect them of being flighty ıd flirty and lacking in depth.

Scorpio with Cancer

This relationship has a lot of sticking power. Neither of these people is interested in short-term partnerships so they'll invest a lot of effort into staying together. The Scorpio will appreciate being looked after so well by their Cancerian. The problem that may arise is if the Scorpio is very secretive and it makes the Cancerian feel threatened.

Scorpio with Leo

It's a dramatic performance when these two get together. They both believe in living life to the full and their relationship won't be without its tempestuous moments. For a start, both of them always believe they're right! But at least their relationship is full of passion—something that they both need if they're to feel completely fulfilled.

Scorpio with Virgo

This couple get on well together and they admire each other's no-nonsense qualities. They're instinctive friends but there are enough differences between them to ensure there's always something to talk about. The Scorpio is intrigued by the contrast between the Virgo modest public image and what happens in private behind the bedroom door.

corpio with Libra

s friends, this unlikely couple will manage to see ıe best in each other. But it's a different story when ıey're lovers because they're chalk and cheese. The corpio is soon irritated by the peace-loving Libran. /hy can't they go ahead and lose their temper once in while? The Scorpio will also be annoyed by the Libran's ısistence on fair play. It spoils the fun!

corpio with Scorpio

oo much of a good thing? It might be when two corpios get together. They understand one another nly too well, which of course has many benefits. motionally, they're on cloud nine. However, there are rawbacks because it's horribly easy for them to absorb ne another's bad moods, so the atmosphere can wiftly turn from sunshine to storms.

corpio with Sagittarius

/hat's going with these two? Probably a lot of ıisunderstandings! This couple are better as friends r business partners than as lovers because their motional needs are so different. The Scorpio will e instantly suspicious if the Sagittarian wants an ıdependent social life. Also, their intense passion will verwhelm the Sagittarian.

Scorpio with Capricorn

It's a strange pairing but it can work! This couple share a need to be seen to do well, so the Scorpio will understand the Capricorn's workaholic tendencies and enjoy the material results. Sexually, it's a pretty earthy combination. The only problem comes if the Scorpio can't encourage the Capricorn to open up emotionally.

Scorpio with Aquarius

This is a tricky one! Although they respect one another's intellects, this couple will struggle to stay together. The Scorpio is resentful and suspicious of the Aquarian's streak of independence because they can't understand or control it. They will also fall out because they're both highly opinionated and utterly convinced that they're in the right!

Scorpio with Pisces

Provided that the Scorpio is ready to show their softer side and the Piscean is keen to develop their tougher side, this couple will be happy together. Problems come if the Piscean is weak-willed and allows the Scorpio to bully them. Nevertheless, they'll both enjoy the intense emotional relationship that develops between them.

Sagittarius

November 23–December 21

THE SAGITTARIUS PERSONALITY

One of the greatest things about a Sagittarian is their irrepressible optimism. Even when things become dice and they start to worry, it won't be long before the Sagittarian begins to feel positive again. This is one of their greatest strengths. Of course, they have their bad days like everyone else. Perhaps this resilient attitude to trouble is the reason that Sagittarius is said to be th luckiest sign in the zodiac!

Jupiter, the planetary ruler of Sagittarius, is the planet of good fortune and challenges. Sagittarius is the third of the Fire signs, which makes its subjects expansive, enthusiastic, and always keen to take the initiative. Although they need to rest every now and then, they aren't happy unless they've got an exciting new project on the go. If they haven't, they will soon start to feel fed up and possibly even depressed.

The sign is symbolized by the Archer shooting his arrows into the air. A typical Sagittarian has always got their eye on a target—usually slightly out of their reach, because where's the fun in achieving somethin simple? A Sagittarian prefers a challenge.

Sagittarians enjoy discussing ideas with friends and loved ones. A Sagittarian is very intellectual, so they love books and have an extremely broad range of knowledge. They spend their lives learning more abou people and the world around them.

A Sagittarian always prides themselves on their honesty. They hate hypocrites, so you can usually expe hear the truth from them. However, this may not ways be a comfortable experience! It doesn't help that little exaggeration often sneaks into a Sagittarian's onversation. Somehow, the Sagittarian version the truth often turns out to be blunter and more rect than you were expecting. It may also involve the agittarian dropping a clanger at the same time. Of all e members of the zodiac, Sagittarians are the ones ost likely to suffer from foot in mouth disease.

OVE

his is one of the most popular signs of the zodiac. agittarians appear to radiate a friendly, easygoing rce-field. In addition to that, they are terrific company.

People appreciate the open and straightforward anner of the Sagittarian because it means they now where they stand. After all, this is not exactly the ost tactful sign in the zodiac so it's awkward for a agittarian to be anything other than honest.

The one thing a Sagittarian can't abide is feeling ed down or hemmed in by a partner. They need to be ble to lead their own life and not feel that someone trying to curb their freedom. They may even end e relationship if that's the only way to maintain a ense of independence. If there are reasons why they an't leave their partner, they will start to distance emselves from them.

Although sex means a lot to a Sagittarian, because allows them a lot of self-expression, the most important requirement when looking for a partner is someone who will be a friend as well as a lover. A Sagittarian needs a partner who'll still be their best friend long after the passion between them has simmered down, and whose intellect matches their own. Anything less simply isn't good enough.

CAREER

This is one of the most intellectual signs in the zodiac, so ideally a Sagittarian should choose a career that gives their brain plenty of scope and, preferably, presents a challenge. Anything that smacks of routine will soon make them feel fed up. Instead, they need an occupation that allows them continually to add to the store of knowledge.

A Sagittarian is a very sociable creature so ideally they need to be surrounded by lively colleagues. They aren't very keen on working alone for long stretches at a time. They are usually popular among their workmates because of their knack of livening up the atmosphere and making people laugh.

A Sagittarian is a born teacher, so if they can impart some of their experience to other people they'll feel satisfied. They also need a job that keeps them on the move and gives them the chance of meeting plenty of interesting people.

Ideal Sagittarian professions include education, publishing, writing, broadcasting, religion, philosophy, and travel. Although Sagittarians are not particularly mbitious, they do like to feel a sense of achievement nd to know that they're getting a lot out of their vork—and also that they're putting a lot into it.

1ONEY

hey love spending money, so they need to earn plenty f it. Unfortunately, they're not very good at taking are of their cash. The Sagittarian will tell themselves hat they've got more important things to think about, lthough they sometimes face a monetary crisis and re forced to take action because something has gone rong with their finances.

As far as most Sagittarians are concerned, the nost exciting thing about money is what it can buy. irtually every Sagittarian loves collecting books. nother important Sagittarian hobby is travel and they ill happily work hard in order to afford adventurous acations to far-flung locations.

Expensive possessions that act as status symbols on't usually appeal to Sagittarians. Most Sagittarians refer wearing casual clothes to anything formal so ren't particularly impressed by designer labels. Even so, ney may be prepared to spend a fortune on beautiful othes made from leather and suede. They also enjoy uying accessories such as gloves, belts, and hats.

Sagittarians often have a weak spot when it omes to fast cars. It probably costs a fortune, too! A agittarian's ideal is to have enough money to be free o do whatever they want with their life.

HEALTH

This is one of the most active signs of all, so a typical Sagittarian enjoys being on the move. Even on days when they don't leave the house or office, they may get plenty of exercise dashing from one room to another.

The more sedentary a Sagittarian's life, the more jittery they feel. They need activities that engage their brain as well as their body. They enjoy walking, although their busy schedule may mean they spend more time in the car or behind a desk than pounding the pavement. They really benefit from being in wide-open spaces and breathing plenty of fresh air. Among the activities that could appeal are horse-riding, squash rackets, motor-racing and any other sport that requires nerves of steel and a daredevil attitude. As a result, a Sagittarian can often strain muscles.

For a Sagittarian, the vulnerable areas of the body are the hips and liver. When they put on weight, it's most likely to center around their hips and can be increasingly hard to shift. They thoroughly enjoy eating and drinking, which means their liver can suffer. They need to balance all those gastronomic binges with a more restrained diet.

:OMPATIBILITY

agittarius with Aries

his couple can look forward to lots of fun and games. hey have a similar outlook on life, both wanting to njoy it as much as possible. They also have plenty of iterests in common. There's always a good-humored ense of competitiveness to their relationship and ey'll love spurring one another on to try new things nd tackle fresh challenges.

agittarius with Taurus

's hard to know what this couple see in each other. he freedom-loving Sagittarian will soon feel stifled by e security-loving Taurean. Any sexual or emotional elationship could soon founder. Even as friends, ey will struggle to understand one another. The agittarian likes to live for today; the Taurean wants to ave for tomorrow.

agittarius with Gemini

hese people are soulmates! They can expect to have emendous fun together, talking about everything nder the Sun. The Sagittarian will encourage the emini to concentrate on things in more depth than ey're used to, and their warm affections will help the emini to relax and be more demonstrative than usual.

Sagittarius with Cancer

There are so many differences between these two that they'll battle to find any common ground. The Sagittarian needs to pull their punches when delivering home truths to the Cancerian, otherwise they'll have to endure a lot of hurt silences. The Sagittarian's need for room to breathe emotionally will confuse the Cancerian

Sagittarius with Leo

This is a terrific combination because these two have a lot in common. They're both very affectionate and demonstrative. They're also very keen to get as much out of life as possible, and will talk one another into all sorts of escapades and adventures. The Sagittarian will gently take the mickey out of the Leo whenever they get too big for their boots.

Sagittarius with Virgo

The major selling point for this partnership is fascination. Both parties are intrigued by one another and there's always plenty to talk about. The only hitch will come if they're so busy talking that they rarely get around to the more intimate aspects of their relationship. However, as friends they really enjoy one another's company.

Capricorn

December 22–January 20

THE CAPRICORN PERSONALITY

People have sometimes dismissed this sign as boring, dull, or too dutiful for words. Well, it's about time all that ended. We may all have met some Capricorns who are full of depressingly bleak pronouncements, such as that the light at the end of the tunnel is an oncoming train but they are not all like that. Usually a Capricorn is the perfect person to turn to in a crisis and they have a wonderful sense of humor.

Another of Capricorn's greatest strengths is the ability to learn from experience. Most of them have their crosses to bear but they usually grit their teeth and get on with it.

Saturn, their planetary ruler, is the planet of hard knocks and tough experiences, so is a hard taskmaster. Saturn rules limitations, and sometimes a Capricorn will seem hidebound and hemmed in by their own lack of confidence. Certainly, some Capricorns are very shy, but as they grow up they usually learn to live with their natural reserve.

Saturn also gives the typical Capricorn a rather pessimistic view of life and the Capricorn can become quite depressed. They may also be quite fearful about the future and need to find a sympathetic listener. That is, provided they are willing to reveal themselves in a vulnerable light.

You see, reputation is very important to Capricorns. Perhaps this is why they often dress quite formally, as though they'll let themselves down if they wear

nything very casual. They like to wear blacks and grays
› they can blend into the background.

Capricorns were born with another wonderful
onus. All the other signs age as they get older, but the
everse happens for Capricorns. As they grow older,
ne normal aging process goes into reverse and they
omehow become younger. They mellow, learn to relax,
nd can be quite skittish by middle age. By the time
d age comes along, they can make teenagers look
ositively boring!

OVE

ne most important thing to remember is that a
apricorn always wants to make a good impression
nd look as though they are in control. Deep down,
ney're extremely shy and vulnerable.

A Capricorn's feelings are easily hurt, even if they
on't let on, and over the years they may learn to
stance themselves emotionally from people as a form
f protection. Yet that doesn't stop them feeling things
eeply, even if they can't bring themselves to show it.
fact, Capricorns aren't noted for their demonstrative
ffections. When rebuffed or rejected, they wonder how
ney will cope. So they try to avoid emotional scenes.
ne Capricorn should make sure their loved ones know
nat they are cared for, even if the Capricorn can't
ways outwardly show it.

Although Capricorns can be quite solitary creatures,
ney benefit tremendously from being in a loving

relationship. Their partner can help them to unwind at the end of a long day and may also encourage them to be more demonstrative and openly affectionate. Even young Capricorns have a rather traditional view of long-term relationships. The men may believe they should be the breadwinners, and the women may want to stay at home and look after the family.

Despite a Capricorn's reserved image, they can be hot stuff in the bedroom—an Earth sign that can be very earthy indeed in the right circumstances!

CAREER

This is where Capricorns really come into their own. They need to be taken seriously and they consider their career to be a way of proving themselves. Yet they may have several false starts. That's because life is often a struggle for Capricorns until they reach their thirtieth birthdays, after which things become much easier.

Whatever a Capricorn's age, their job is very important to them because they need to prove that they can make their own way through life. They're extremely ambitious and may have secret plans about heading straight for the top of their particular tree. What's more they stand an excellent chance of succeeding.

At work, a Capricorn is an invaluable member of a team, thanks to their diligence, pragmatism, and patience. Bosses and colleagues know they can rely on the Capricorn to get things done. This strong sense of duty can keep a Capricorn chained to their esk long after everyone else has gone home. Their ımily life may suffer, but the Capricorn still can't nagine behaving in any other way. This means that Capricorn without a goal in life is a very sorry sight. they are out of work for long they will soon become epressed and lacking in self-confidence.

Among the professions that are ideally suited to a apricorn are big business, dentistry, osteopathy, the vil service, and government work. They cope well with esponsible jobs, and even if it is lonely at the top they'll e able to manage beautifully.

1ONEY

apricorns have a healthy respect for money and what can buy. It's no coincidence that there are many kes about the Capricorn streak of meanness. They ertainly don't like to fritter money away, although they an be surprisingly open-handed when making major urchases. Mind you, the Capricorn will still be reluctant part with small amounts of cash.

Money also means a lot to a Capricorn because offers them material and emotional security and, ierefore, the respect of others. These are the essential ıgredients of a Capricorn's happiness and they will el something is missing if they don't have all three. ne Capricorn will be reluctant to get married or start a ımily until they know they can afford to do so.

When investing that hard-earned cash, a Capricorn ees to buy things that will last a long time. Generally speaking, fads and fashions pass them by because the Capricorn knows these won't last so there is no point i wasting money on them. They have a natural affinity with big business so may become interested in dabblir in the stock market, but only if there's little risk of losing their shirt.

HEALTH

Capricorns will worry about anything given half the chance. It can lead to sleepless nights, poor digestion, and a persistent sense of impending doom.

This is partly because Capricorns have such a strong sense of responsibility. Learning to relax properly has a dramatic impact on their energy levels and will also improve their sleeping patterns. If a Capricorn finds it hard to unwind, they should get involved in a hobby that will allow them to keep active while engaging the mind—gardening suits them well, because contact witl the ground complements their Earth element. Howeve yet again, they need to combat the nagging feeling that they can't knock off for the day until they've eradicated every weed from the garden.

The body's skeletal structure is ruled by Capricorn, so members of this sign need to take care of their bones in general and their knees in particular. Ideally, they should live in a warm, dry climate. Unfortunately, Capricorns can be susceptible to arthritis, so they should take plenty of gentle exercise. They can also have problems with their teeth.

OMPATIBILITY

apricorn with Aries

ıese people are very good for each other! The Arien ›aches the Capricorn not to take life so seriously and › relax more. Even so, there is an element of friendly ›mpetition, especially in their careers, that can lead › success for both of them and a very comfortable andard of living.

apricorn with Taurus

ıis partnership places a big emphasis on security. ›th signs like to feel safe in a relationship and to know ıat their hearts won't be broken. If anything, this ›uple can appear to be rather conservative and staid, ›rhaps with the relationship seeming old-fashioned. ›t it's probably pretty spicy when they're in private!

apricorn with Gemini

ıis is often a short-lived relationship because these ›ople have little in common. The Capricorn will ıjoy being around the lively Gemini but their heavy orkload may eventually spoil things between them. ıey're good friends because they're able to enjoy their ›ofound differences rather than struggle to surmount ıem in a romantic relationship.

Capricorn with Cancer

Here's a relationship that can happily stand the test of time and will become stronger as the years roll by. Both people need emotional security and they'll work hard to make one another feel safe. The Capricorn may eve be encouraged to be more openly demonstrative. They can let their guard down with a Cancerian.

Capricorn with Leo

Both signs place a lot of importance on outward appearances, so occasionally this partnership may be all style and little substance. They are often happier as business partners than as lovers, because they both have a healthy respect for money. The Capricorn can work away behind the scenes while the confident Leo fronts the operation.

Capricorn with Virgo

This is a relationship where both partners know where they stand. And that's exactly how they like it because neither of them wants to waste their time or be left guessing about outcomes. Their partnership may seem to be lacking in open affection and, as time goes on, it can come to resemble more of a business relationship than an emotional one.

apricorn with Libra

though these two have enough in common to bring iem together, it may not be enough to keep them gether for long. The Capricorn may find that the bran isn't assertive enough and will soon be irritated ' their desire to find the happy medium whenever ossible. They'll do better as friends or colleagues.

apricorn with Scorpio

erything goes on underneath the surface with this uple. They will give the impression of being rather etached and distant but there will be some hot nd heavy scenes in private. They both enjoy a high andard of living and will work hard to achieve it. is may mean that their relationship places a lot of nphasis on money.

apricorn with Sagittarius

isn't exactly plain sailing when these two pair up. ey may well hit squalls if the Capricorn disapproves of e Sagittarian's lifestyle or wants them to spend more me at home. On the plus side, however, there will be enty of laughter and the Capricorn may learn to be ore relaxed and less uptight. Even so, the relationship quires lots of hard slog.

Capricorn with Capricorn

At last a Capricorn has found someone who understands them! The question is whether they're to similar. Ideally, they should both appreciate their hom comforts, otherwise they'll spend all their spare time working and will never see one another. As business partners, they make a formidable team. Watch out, world when two Capricorns get together!

Capricorn with Aquarius

This is a strange combination because they're so different. The Capricorn has a sentimental attachmen to tradition while the Aquarian wants to sweep it awa and deal with the facts. So will this relationship work? They need to find some common ground otherwise they'll wind each other up and become infuriated with one another.

Capricorn with Pisces

This can work, provided the Capricorn brings out their innate kindness and the Piscean displays their common sense. They have a lot to teach each other. The Capricorn sees that it's acceptable to be emotiona and the Piscean learns to be more self-reliant. Even so, they will have to work hard and be prepared to make allowances for one another.

Aquarius

January 21—February 19

THE AQUARIUS PERSONALITY

You have to remember that Aquarians are completely different from every other sign. To an Aquarian, it may take years before they fit in with the people around them or even feel comfortable about being so nonconformist. The typical Aquarian approaches life from a very different perspective to most people.

Uranus, the planetary ruler of Aquarius, is responsible for this originality. This planet works in unpredictable and erratic ways. For a start, it makes them totally independent. They follow the beat of a different drum and need to go their own way through life. Loved ones who try to stop them or hold them ba will soon discover how useless this effort is.

This is a good reminder of one of the principal Aquarian characteristics—stubbornness verging on obstinacy. Even if their decision is inconvenient for everyone else, or possibly even offensive, they still won budge. However, they're very hard to predict, so they'll probably take you by complete surprise.

Usually, the present is of much more interest to an Aquarian than the past. They also have their finger on the pulse of the future. As a result, they can seem like iconoclasts, possibly even a threat, because they have revolutionary theories or swim against the tide o popular ideas. Not that this bothers them!

As the third of the Air signs, Aquarians operate on a predominantly mental level. This makes them extremely intelligent and tremendously rational—

en to the exasperation of the people around them o tend to take a more emotional approach to life. uarians are capable of distancing themselves from uations so they can view them objectively. This kes them seem quite dispassionate, and possibly n heartless, but it means they don't get swept along emotion or sentiment.

VE

uarius is the friendliest sign in the zodiac. They value ir friends highly and they need to know that they're und, even if they don't get together very often.

When it comes to loving relationships, it's vital for Aquarian to choose a lover who is also a friend. They y even realize that the most important relationships heir life begin as friendships, with love only arriving erward. It's very hard for an Aquarian to love neone if they don't like them too.

It's also important for an Aquarian to find a partner ose intellect matches their own, so they've always fresh subjects to discuss. The Aquarian will quickly bored if the conversation never progresses past at was on television last night.

An Aquarian's partner must also understand and pect their need for independence. This doesn't mean Aquarian wants to sleep with everyone they meet— y're far too loyal and honest for that—but it does an they hate to think someone wants to know their ry move. It would soon make them feel stifled and

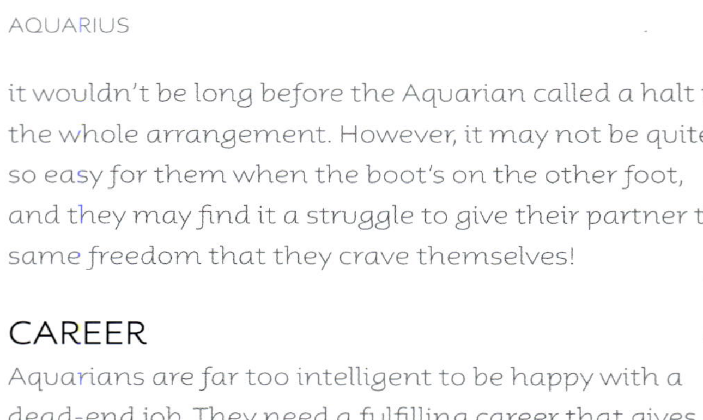

it wouldn't be long before the Aquarian called a halt t the whole arrangement. However, it may not be quite so easy for them when the boot's on the other foot, and they may find it a struggle to give their partner t same freedom that they crave themselves!

CAREER

Aquarians are far too intelligent to be happy with a dead-end job. They need a fulfilling career that gives them plenty to think about. Many Aquarians make a success of their careers but this may be more by accident than design. Instead, their wholehearted involvement and strong intellect ensures they're noticed by people who can help them make it to the top. Their streak of originality helps to make them stand out from the crowd.

Ideally, an Aquarian's career should draw on their tremendous humanitarian instincts—they might be attracted to charity or social work. They can't stand t idea of living off the efforts of others, so they shy awa from any job that obviously exploits people or that go against their strong principles. However, they aren't averse to making money if they think they've earned

Being self-employed is ideal for an Aquarian. They have all the motivation and determination needed to ensure they get the work done in time. Being confronted by someone in charge often brings out the Aquarian's rebellious streak! And it's even worse i they think the person in authority doesn't know wha ey're doing or is only in it for the money. It's not sy for an Aquarian to take orders from other people, cause they think they could do their job so much tter. And they're probably absolutely right!

ONEY

uarians have a love-hate relationship with money. ey relish occasional bouts of extravagance, but hate e way this involves them in a consumer-led society.

Provided they have enough to keep a roof over eir head and food on their plate, why should they ed a lot of cash in the bank? Unfortunately this itude doesn't always go down very well with partners d family because it can lead to misunderstanding d resentment, especially if everyone suspects the uarian is out of touch with the cost of living.

Humanitarianism runs through an Aquarian like ters through a stick of seaside rock, and they are ually happy to help out anyone in financial trouble. t very often charity begins at home for them. The uarian may make a point of never giving to charity cause they say the charities don't spend the money the right things, but they will happily bail out a end or relative who's up against it.

Although an Aquarian will keep a close eye on e day-to-day management of their bank account, ey're not very interested in high finance. They detest vesting in large companies whose business practices e harming the environment or exploiting people.

HEALTH

Because an Aquarian's energies tend to operate in an erratic way, it's very important for them to take steady and regular exercise. Alternating long periods inactivity with sweaty bursts of exertion is a recipe fo disaster. Pounding away in the gym or jogging throug fume-filled streets isn't an Aquarian's idea of fun. Far better to find an activity that allows them to exercise their body and relax their mind—like yoga, Pilates, or Qi Gong. They also benefit from meditation, especiall if they can do it with other people.

An Aquarian understands the importance of a healthy diet and is probably very sympathetic toward the idea of vegetarianism, if not veganism too. Orgar foods also appeal to them and they may even grow their own fruit and vegetables. Food-combining or macrobiotics can attract them too and will suit their sensitive system. However, it's important that the Aquarian doesn't become so stubborn and dogmatic about this that they refuse to relax the rules and thereby cause offense. They can also become unwell i they follow an extreme diet. When they are ill, they m respond well to complementary medicine because th like the holistic approach that's involved.

An Aquarian's circulation and ankles are the two most vulnerable areas of their body. They should mak sure their ankles are well-supported whenever they exercise. Regular exercise will help keep their circulati working efficiently.

ƆMPATIBILITY

uarius with Aries

is combination is good fun, especially as friends. ither sign is scared to say what they think, so they'll ve some good-humored but fierce debates. The only al snag comes if the Aquarian's emotions are too cool the hot-blooded Arien. The Aquarian may also be armed at first, but then subsequently irritated, by the en's naïveté.

uarius with Taurus

is couple will struggle to stay together as they have little in common. They also have very different ways ooking at the world. The Aquarian will soon be strated by the Taurean's need to cling to the status o, and will feel bemused by the Taurean's slightly ssessive attitude. Why can't they lighten up? the uarian wonders.

uarius with Gemini

hatever the nature of this couple's relationship, it will ve a strongly intellectual slant. They'll love talking out virtually every subject under the Sun, and the uarian will teach the Gemini to think things through more detail and without leaping to easy conclusions. th of them benefit from this alliance.

Aquarius with Cancer

This is a mystifying pairing. It's hard to imagine what will bring them together in the first place, let alone keep them together! The Aquarian will soon tire of th way the Cancerian lives on their emotions, and will fe suffocated by the care and attention that's constantl being lavished on them. They must each make plenty of allowances for one another.

Aquarius with Leo

This is great fun! The Aquarian admires the Leo's style and self-confidence, although they find it hard to cope with their tendency to turn a snag into a drama. Emotionally, they have a lot to learn from the affectionate Leo, who will encourage them to be more open about their feelings and more demonstrative.

Aquarius with Virgo

As friends, this couple have plenty of differences but they can surmount them. As lovers, they could quickly come unstuck. Neither sign is renowned for being emotional or demonstrative and this is where probler start. Their relationship could soon become rather distant and sterile, with neither of them knowing hov to reach out and bridge the gap.

uarius with Libra

is is one of the best combinations for an Aquarian. ey marvel at the Libran's tact, enjoy their considerate ture and appreciate their agile brain. They will also joy teasing the Libran and watching them rise to e bait! This couple are great friends, good business rtners, and happy lovers, so they win all round.

uarius with Scorpio

hat do you get when you put two of the most gmatic signs together? Stalemate! Differences of inion will spring up all the time, with neither person anting to back down. Problems over the Aquarian's ed for independence will drive a wedge between em, with the Aquarian ultimately feeling trapped d manipulated.

uarius with Sagittarius

re are two people who both need to go their own ay but there's no danger of them drifting apart—the ry fact that their partner gives them plenty of scope ll keep them together. They'll enjoy fascinating nversations about all sorts of things because neither gn is a dunce. They will also share a deep love for one other, based on mutual respect.

Aquarius with Capricorn

Give and take is needed on both sides if this relationship is to work. The iconoclastic Aquarian mu appreciate the Capricorn's conservative attitude, and the Capricorn must learn to relax more. They're great as business partners because their combined gifts create an unstoppable team. But as lovers, they don't know what to make of one another.

Aquarius with Aquarius

This could be a marriage of true minds or it could be a recipe for disaster! Provided each Aquarian is willing to listen to their partner, their relationship will flourish. But if each one insists that only their opinion counts and their partner is talking rubbish, they will be heading for trouble. Sexually, it will be great or gruesome. There's no happy medium.

Aquarius with Pisces

This relationship has all the makings of a mismatch. The Aquarian can't understand why the Piscean is so sensitive and easily hurt, and the Piscean thinks the Aquarian is so strange that they must have come fror another planet. They aren't natural friends but they'll eventually forge a bond. A love affair, however, will be much harder work.

Pisces

February 20–March 20

THE PISCES PERSONALITY

Pisces is the last of the twelve signs of the zodiac and it's said to contain a little of each of the other eleven signs. No one knows whether that's true, but Pisces is certainly the sign of the saint or the sinner. The symb or glyph, for Pisces represents two fish swimming in opposite directions, and this describes the way Pisces can hit the heights or sink to the lowest depths.

It can be very difficult for a Piscean to keep their feet on the ground. This is because they are ruled by the mystical, spiritual planet Neptune. And their Water element means they are easily swayed by their emotions and are quckly moved to tears.

The result is that Pisces is the sign of the dreamer, the visionary, and the saint, but it can also be the sign of the fantasist and the criminal. Some Pisceans can talk themselves into almost anything.

Pisceans have an almost bottomless reservoir of compassion for other people, even when they suspect they are being conned by them. Many Pisceans will work hard for their favorite charity or for a local good cause, although you may never know anything about

Many Pisceans say they go through life in a dream. As teenagers they don't have a chosen career and the feel at the mercy of whatever fate has to offer them.

Pisceans have an instinctive dislike of unpleasant situations or harsh facts. This may simply mean that they're reluctant to watch violent films or read unsavory articles in the newspapers. The results of this

aracteristic can be disastrous, because it means they
n turn a blind eye to trouble until it's unavoidable—
d too late to do anything about it. If a Piscean wants
oe truly happy, they must learn to temper their need
peace and harmony with an ability to face up to life
it really is, warts and all.

)VE

s a rare Piscean who can separate their emotions
m their daily life. A Piscean often wears their heart
their sleeve. This makes them a born romantic
: also very sensitive and vulnerable. Sometimes,
ey may even see slights where none exists, or allow
eir imagination to work overtime so they dream up
entire incident with someone. It also means they
e extremely emotional, and they pour out love and
ection to their favorite people. If the Piscean is lucky,
eir loved ones are able to respond in kind or to accept
eir love without feeling overwhelmed. Even so, the
cean should try to keep their feelings in check if they
reaten to spiral out of control too often. Some signs
nply can't cope with a lot of highly charged drama
d the Piscean will feel hurt if their partner tunes out.

Most Pisceans are faithful but some have a capacity
deception, and they seem so thoroughly nice that
one would suspect they're busy juggling their string
overs. It's all part of the Piscean duality.

It's natural for a Piscean to see the best in other
ople, which is one of the reasons they have so many

admirers. Even if everyone else can see that their late love is no good for them, the Piscean will persist in ignoring their faults and trusting that love will find a way. When it does, they're deliriously happy. When it doesn't, they sink to the depths of despair.

CAREER

Pisceans are drawn to professions that are either incredibly glamorous and artistic or which involve the being of service to others and are therefore incredibly unglamorous!

The film industry is ruled by Neptune, the ruler of Pisces, and many members of this sign are photographers, actors, dancers, choreographers, and designers. Pisceans are also attracted to the perfume cosmetics, and fashion businesses. You'll also find mo Pisceans running drinking clubs and bars, or working breweries. They may also be involved in the oil industr

Many Pisceans devote their lives to looking after others, especially in institutions such as hospitals, hospices, and prisons. The contemplative life of a religious order can also appeal to Pisceans. At the oth extreme, there are plenty of Pisceans living on the wrong side of the law.

Wherever a Piscean works, they need a sympathet atmosphere, pleasant surroundings, and colleagues who appreciate them. Any job where they're nothing more than a drudge will quickly depress them and m eventually make them ill. Pisces is one of the most

ative signs of all, so ideally a Piscean should be able express this side of their nature. They also have a werful imagination which needs a constructive tlet, otherwise it might play games with them. If ey can't put these artistic gifts to use in their job, they ould make sure they express them in their spare ne, otherwise they will soon feel very frustrated.

ONEY

ces and money go together like oil and water, pecially when it comes to the routine day-to-day anagement of a Piscean's finances. A typical Piscean ncentrates most of their energy on creative activities her than materialistic ones. They may find it difficult keep track of where all the money goes, or might get o a real state whenever it's time to tackle their taxes. e best answer to this is either to pay a trustworthy countant to handle their finances for them, or to grit eir teeth and tackle things sooner rather than later.

Although a Piscean is prone at times to dreaming of vonderfully lavish lifestyle, they are probably perfectly ppy if they have enough money to live on, preferably h a little left over to give to their loved ones. All the ne, it's a good idea for them to set aside any spare sh for a rainy day or a big treat, but they should get und, independent financial advice. Because most ceans are so trusting, it's easy for sharks and con en to get the better of them, so they should be very utious when investing their money.

If a Piscean happens to be rich, they like to live in the most luxurious and extravagant way possible. They'll able to live out all their fantasies.

HEALTH

Emotions and health often go hand in hand, and a Piscean's well-being can be powerfully affected by their feelings. If they are unhappy, it can show in their body, perhaps through a chill or a cold. Stress can present particular problems for a Piscean because it can play havoc with their finely tuned nervous system triggering such symptoms as headaches, stomach upsets, and sleepless nights. It's important for a Piscean to take immense care of themselves, making sure they don't skimp on meals and that they get plenty of rest. Whenever they feel particularly vulnerable, they should try to keep away from tense or unpleasant atmospheres because they can absorb negative vibrations like a psychic sponge.

The feet are the most vulnerable area of the body for a Piscean, so they may suffer from corns, chilblains or struggle to find shoes that fit properly. Whenever they become tense, they'll feel better if they treat themselves to a pedicure or give themselves a foot massage. Walking on grass with bare feet can help to ground them. Swimming is a marvelous way for them to combine exercise and relaxation. They may be allergic to certain foods or drugs, and often respond well to complementary medicines.

)MPATIBILITY

ces with Aries

spite initial fascination between two people who profoundly different, this relationship will struggle survive. There is simply too big a gap between them. ey are much happier as friends than lovers because Arien will soon become frustrated with the dreamy cean who prefers romance to raunchy lust.

ces with Taurus

ere's a lot of mutual empathy and understanding in s relationship. They have a similar approach to life d love because they both crave emotional security. wever, the Piscean may sometimes find the Taurean ather too literal and prosaic for their taste, but they y be able to encourage them to loosen up and be re imaginative in time.

ces with Gemini

ally, this couple should be friends or business rtners rather than lovers. Although they have ny interests in common, their emotional eds are so different that these will soon lead to sunderstandings. The Piscean wishes the Gemini re more demonstrative and less scared of showing ir feelings, but may be unable to say so.

Pisces with Cancer

These are two of the most sensitive signs of the zodic so they feel safe when they get together. At least they know they won't be deliberately hurt. In fact, they mc go out of their way to protect each other's feelings, ar this can lead to hitches if they feel incapable of talkir problems through in case they upset the apple cart.

Pisces with Leo

This is an uneasy combination and definitely one tha stands a better chance of success if it's platonic rathe than passionately physical. The Piscean will adore helping the Leo to enjoy the good life but after a while they may feel rather harried by the Leo's tendency to organize them and boss them about. This is less likely to happen if they're just friends.

Pisces with Virgo

Opposites usually attract but in this case they can repel. At first, the Piscean likes the Virgo's no-nonsens attitude and ability to bail them out of trouble, but after a while it can start to grate. They may even unconsciously become more disorganized in order to annoy the Virgo! They will also feel hurt by the Virgo's typical nagging and criticism.

ces with Libra

romance all the way when these two get together. ey will put a lot of effort into keeping their ationship as fresh and exciting as when it began. wever, this can cause problems if neither person nts to face up to the inevitable difficulties that arise ny relationship. They both have to be prepared to kle the bad times as well as enjoy the good ones.

ces with Scorpio

otion flows thick and fast between this couple. As nds, they'll talk for hours about their relationships l swap stories. As lovers, they'll enjoy a partnership t seethes with drama and sizzles with sensation. rything between them will be conducted at a ghtened level, which is exactly the way that both of m like it.

ces with Sagittarius

s works as a friendship because these people have ough in common to keep them talking for hours. ey may also share a religious or spiritual quest. But ngs can get dicey if they fall in love because there is much scope for crossed wires and hurt feelings, with Piscean bearing the brunt of the pain.

Pisces with Capricorn

Although they may seem like chalk and cheese, this couple manage to get on well together, provided the Piscean isn't too unworldly. The Piscean admires the Capricorn's head for business and their capacity for hard work, and the Capricorn likes the Piscean's intuition and sensitivity. They will both do their best t make their home a cosy and safe place.

Pisces with Aquarius

These people come from different worlds and can't make head nor tail of each other. They will get by as friends, although it will take a lot of spade work to reach that point, but will encounter many problems i an emotional relationship. Their needs are so dissim that they will struggle to understand one another.

Pisces with Pisces

This is a great partnership because neither Piscean has to explain themselves to anyone. Sometimes the may even be no need for words because there is such a depth of shared understanding. Yet this can lead to sticky patches because both Pisceans will allow their imaginations to run away with them if they don't ha the facts to keep their feet on the ground.

NOTES